# Best Restaurants® Philadelphia
## & Environs

# Elaine Tait

101 Productions
San Francisco

Best Restaurants is the trademark of 101 Publishing Company, Inc., registered with the United States Patent and Trademarks Office.

Published by 101 Productions
834 Mission Street
San Francisco, California 94103
Distributed to the book trade in the United States
by Charles Scribner's Sons, New York.

*Library of Congress Cataloging in Publication Data*

Tait, Elaine.
    Best restaurants, Philadelphia & environs.

    Includes index.
    1. Philadelphia--Restaurants--Directories.   I. Title.
TX907.T34          647'.95748'11          79-12551
ISBN  0-89286-150-9

# Contents

# Introduction

Sixteen years ago, when I became food editor and restaurant critic for *The Philadelphia Inquirer,* there were simply not enough good local restaurants to fill a guide book. Today, a guide to dining out in the Philadelphia area is not only possible, it is essential.

We have a full range of ethnic restaurants now. You could, for example, explore each of China's many cuisines without ever leaving the few square blocks of Chinatown here. Or taste your way through Italy, Thailand, Greece, France, India, Mexico, Ireland, Spain, Portugal, Germany, Vietnam and even Morocco . . . all within the city limits.

Philadelphia now has luxury-class restaurants that consistently rate with the best anywhere. We have excellent steak and seafood restaurants, a gourmet cafeteria, a food bazaar (in a downtown shopping mall) as well as restaurants in art galleries, gardens, cookware and antique shops, ships and chic cellars.

And, of course, we have our storefronts, those small, happy restaurants furnished with hanging plants, love, imagination and very little money. Storefront chefs refuse to settle for menu clichés. They mix and marry cuisines marvelously. While this makes for great dining excitement, it also makes it difficult for the guidebook writer attempting to categorize their style. Calling it "international," which I've done here, tells only a part of the story. I think of it as "Nouvelle Philadelphia."

As the area's longest-playing restaurant critic, I was a witness to the birth of Philadelphia as a major restaurant city. I may have even helped things happen by encouraging promising talent and making hamburger out of some sacred cows. From the very beginning, I told of the tough, the ersatz and the overpriced as well as the tender, the prime and the perfectly lovely.

What I wrote occasionally brought "how could you? " looks from the paper's advertising sales staff, nasty letters from restaurant owners and, once, a rock through my living room window. It also brought readers' trust. Then, as now, my review partner and I arrived unannounced, ate without calling attention to our mission, paid the check and left quietly, giving the restaurant no opportunity to attempt to beg, flatter or bribe their way to a favorable write up.

Those restaurants I consider best from my years of reviewing are included in this book. Let me say, however, that you are still the real judge of the "best" restaurant for you.

To help you make that judgement, this book includes menus and prices in effect at the date of publication. Both are subject to change at any time and should be taken as relative guides.

Calculations were based on the cost of an average dinner with appetizer, entrée, dessert and coffee. Drinks, tax and tip were not included.

# RATING SYMBOLS

**$**    **UNDER $10** Some of the restaurants in this category dish out large portions but don't give much in the way of ambience. Some don't go overboard on portions but let you enjoy a little candlelight and romance with your budget meal. Go prepared for the limitations.

**$$**    **UNDER $20** A majority of the restaurants in the book fall in this range. For the money you should expect interesting, well-prepared food and a pleasant setting.

**$$$**    **OVER $20** For this amount you should get top-quality ingredients, expert preparation and service and a luxurious setting.

# Philadelphia

## Philadelphia: Center City
## ARTHUR'S
Steaks $$$

Arthur's has always seemed like a man's restaurant to me, a steak palace where the setting usually played second fiddle to the sirloin. That's why a recent meal here with a woman friend proved such a pleasant surprise. They've brightened the place up since my first visit years ago and while the decor isn't flowery and feminine it's lively and unlike the smoky, drab room I remembered. The biggest boost comes from walls covered with what appears to be handwoven wool in an American Indian design. Arthur's doesn't confuse you with fancy or fussy dishes. The appetizers are all old favorites like chopped liver, herring, bacon-wrapped chicken livers, clams on the half shell and shrimp cocktail. Two entrées tested and approved were a small sirloin steak and calves liver with bacon. The steak was sizzling hot and cooked perfectly (I ordered it medium-rare). It was slightly, but not unpleasantly, chewy and the flavor was full and natural. With it was a serving of nutmeg-spiced, creamed spinach and giant, piping hot French fries. The two large pieces of calves liver were garnished with lots of crisp, delicious bacon slices and accompanied with a big baked potato and creamed spinach. The liver was so palatable that when the portion proved too much for my friend's modest appetite, she toted the rest home in a people bag. In addition to salads, diners here get crisp, crunchy dill pickles and good dark bread and rolls.

ARTHUR'S STEAK HOUSE, 1512 Walnut Street, Philadelphia. Telephone: (215) 735-2590. Lunch: Monday-Friday 11-3. Dinner: Monday-Friday 3-11; Saturday 4-12. Late supper after 10 pm. Closed Sunday and holidays. Cards: AE, DC, MC, VISA. Reservations advised. Full bar service. Nearby parking garages.

# appetizers

Cherrystone clams on the half shell $2.25
Herring with sour cream and onions $1.50
Mushroom caps stuffed with crabmeat $3.25
Chopped chicken livers $2.00
Shrimp cocktail $4.95
Chicken livers wrapped in bacon $2.25

# soups

Baked onion $1.75
Snapper $1.75
Soup du Jour $1.25

# entrees

All entrees come with the special touch that has made Arthur's a landmark in Philadelphia dining.
Included are dinner rolls and our special rye and pumpernickel breads. Lettuce and tomato salad with
choice of dressing. (Excluding Roquefort)
Delicious pickles, vegetable and special French fries or baked Idaho potato.

**Steaks** We list our steaks separately because they are our specialty.
Prime sirloin $13.25
Small sirloin $11.50
Prime filet mignon $13.25
Chateaubriand for two $28.00
Rib steak with garlic $12.00
Broiled chopped sirloin $7.25

Roast prime ribs of beef $10.50
Broiled pork chops $7.75
Broiled calves liver $7.75

Roast Long Island duck, orange sauce, and fruit stuffing $8.75
Boneless breast of chicken (chef's choice) $7.50

Broiled lobster tail $13.00
Broiled fresh flounder $7.50
Broiled fresh flounder stuffed with crab meat $9.75
Broiled brook trout, almondine $7.50
Baked Alaskan king crab imperial $9.75
Sauteed scallops in lemon, butter sauce $7.95

# specials

**The Original** $5.50
A thick tenderloin steak served on rye bread
with our delicious French fries. It's made us
famous.
**Potato Pancakes (A.K.A.) Latkes** $3.25
Pan fried, crisp and delicious. This specialty is a
classic. Served with sour cream or apple sauce.

# salads

Caesar salad (for two) $4.00
Mixed green salad $1.75
Spinach salad $2.50
Anchovies, sliced tomato,
  onions and pimentos $2.75
Lettuce and sliced tomato $1.25
Roquefort dressing $.75 extra

# Philadelphia: Center City
## ASTRAL PLANE
### International

$$

The glasses are recycled sour cream jars. The "silver" doesn't match, but then neither do the china place settings, the chairs or the table linens. Overhead there's a draped parachute. Underfoot, the floor is patched and unpolished. On the table, there's a tiny bouquet of fresh flowers and a non-functioning electric clock lamp with a brass drum majorette sunning herself in the 25-watt glow. Is this a serious restaurant or an exercise in shoestring decorating? After almost seven years of doing business at the address, Astral Plane seems to qualify as the former. At 5:45 on a weekday evening, we were the first arrivals in the small downstairs dining room. (There's a greenhouse room out back and a bar as you enter.) By dessert and coffee time, courting couples of mixed and matching sexes, neighborhood loners and a happy-noisy party of four had been tucked into every cozy corner. The Astral Plane menu is small enough to be handled easily by the tiny kitchen. One of the excellent appetizers consists of shrimp wrapped in thin, spring-roll skins, then deep fried so crisp they crackle at the touch of a tooth. An accompanying sauce has an agreeable snap of ginger to it. Entrées are eclectic and might on any evening range from honey-sweetened chicken curry with fruit to Thai-style pork. The dessert selection is limited but choice. Among the excellent offerings is a European-type chocolate cake that is dark, dense and delicious. Coffee is cinnamon scented.

ASTRAL PLANE, 1708 Lombard Street, Philadelphia. Telephone: (215) 546-6230. Lunch: Monday-Friday 12-2:30. Dinner: Monday-Thursday 5:30-11; Friday and Saturday to 12:30 am; Sunday noon-11 pm. Cards: AE, MC, VISA. Reservations are advised, particularly for Friday lunch, and are required for Friday and Saturday dinner. Full bar service. Street parking.

**Philadelphia: East Philly**
**BANGKOK HOUSE**
**Thai**                                                    **$**

Bangkok House offers the fascinating food of Thailand in a neat setting smack dab in the middle of Philadelphia's restaurant-renaissance area. Asterisks beside menu items tell how hot and spicy a dish will be. A no-asterisk dish like koon gra tieam prig-Thai can be fairly subtle (if shrimp sauced with garlic and pepper can be said to be subtle under any circumstances.) Yum num tok, a cold roast beef salad with hot pepper, cucumber and lemon juice, is just the opposite—a real tongue tingler. In between there are spicy compromises like tom yum koong, a soup that floats shrimp and lemon grass (it looks like bits of hay), and rose-leaf sized kaffirlime leaves that have a vague citrus taste. Whatever you order will taste milder tempered with steamed rice. Jasmine tea also helps cool things off. Thai desserts here are exotic canned fruits. We sampled the lychee and rambutan and found both interesting in texture but about as flavorful as American canned fruits.

BANGKOK HOUSE, 117 South Street, Philadelphia. Telephone: (215) 925-0655. Hours: Tuesday-Sunday 5:30 pm-11:30 pm. Closed Monday. Cards: AE, MC, VISA. Reservations accepted. No alcoholic beverages; bring your own wine or beer. Street parking.

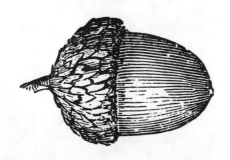

## BLACK BANANA
French                                         $$

Black Banana was Banane Noire when it introduced Phila-
delphians to a new style of restaurant. Squeezed into a tiny,
glass-fronted former store in a neighborhood that was in the
process of being reclaimed by artists and craftsmen, it
offered flea-market decor and experimental food prepared
and served by local free spirits. With prosperity, the restau-
rant outgrew its first home, changed its name to Black
Banana and its address to another neighborhood moving
rapidly towards expensive fashionability. There's now a
choice of settings: neon-spiffy art moderne downstairs or
cozy belle epoque upstairs. And food that, following cur-
rent fashion, shows the seasonings and sauces of nouvelle
cuisine. Chef Xavier Hussenet has a passion for finding the
freshest seasonal ingredients. In autumn, he'll present snails
with sweet wine and chestnuts, duckling with seasonal
fruits. Fresh crayfish are on the menu when they're avail-
able, and there is always a freshly caught Atlantic fish
selection. The wine list includes some interesting California
choices as well as French wines.

BLACK BANANA, 247 Race Street, Philadelphia. Tele-
phone: (215) 925-4433. Hours: daily 6 pm-2 am. All major
cards. Reservations advised. Full bar service. Street parking.

Clear oxtail soup
Cream of white beans and chicken livers
Tossed California lettuces with house dressing
Cold marinated shrimp and crab with tropical fruit
Slivers of salmon spiced with coriander and salt cod
Cold pâté with layers of fresh vegetables and ham
Baked snails flavoured with Muscadet and chestnuts


Atlantic coast catch of the day
Brazilian crayfish in Fernand Point's recipe


Chicken breasts braised in greens with Madeira sauce
Duckling with autumn vine ripe fruit
Cutlet from rack of veal with lemon, tomatoes, garlic...
Prime center cut sirloin with green peppercorns
Loin of porc in a fennel and cream reduction
Marinated rack of lamb accompanied by Indian chutney

Inquire about our daily special; not served on Saturday

# BLUE POINT
Seafood                                             $

From the street, the Blue Point could double for a truck stop. From the front door, you'd swear you were entering a fish store. From behind a filled plate, however, a table at the Blue Point should look a little like heaven. Hard-shell crabs are a specialty, but the price is also right for mussels, clams, oysters and just about anything else that wears armor plate and lives in salt water. You can take your pick of raw, steamed, sauced or stylishly embellished versions. Ask for steamed little necks and get a dozen of the sweetest nuggets of clam flesh imaginable. The clams casino arrive seasoned with bacon and chopped vegetables. The hardshells are so fresh and lively tasting, it's difficult to believe a superhighway and not some crustacean-rich sea water inlet is out the back door. The crabs, cool in temperature, hot in seasoning, disappear quickly, the shell fragments adding to the mountain of debris that accumulates at each place. Corn on the cob is as close as the Blue Point gets to an accompaniment. Cooked just enough, the corn offers a surprising taste of summer no matter what the season. Cold beer is always available.

BLUE POINT CRAB HOUSE AND RESTAURANT, Harbison Avenue and Tulip Street, Philadelphia. Telephone: (215) 743-8838. Hours: Monday-Thursday 10 am-midnight; Friday and Saturday to 1 am; Sunday noon-9 pm. No cards. No reservations. Beer only. Street parking.

# MENU

| FROM OUR MODERN STEAM TABLE | | | | PRICE |
|---|---|---|---|---|
| MUSSELS | 1 ORDER (A BOWL) | $ 2.00 |
| LITTLE NECKS | 1 ORDER (A BOWL) | 2.50 |
| OYSTERS | 1 DOZEN | 3.50 |
| IPSWITCH (with butter sauce) 1 ORDER (A BOWL) | 2.75 |
| CORN ON THE COB | .75 |
| CLAMS CASINO | 6 TO AN ORDER | 1.75 |
| OYSTER ROCKEFELLER (6 TO AN ORDER) | 2.00 |
| MUSSELS IN RED SAUCE | (A BOWL) | 2.75 |
| MUSSELS IN WHITE SAUCE | (" " ) | 2.75 |
| LITTLE NECKS IN RED SAUCE | (A BOWL) | 2.75 |
| LITTLE NECKS IN WHITE SAUCE | (A BOWL) | 2.75 |
| WHOLE LOBSTER (SOLD BY WEIGHT) | 5.00 |
| KING CRAB LEGS (WITH BUTTER SAUCE) | 6.00 |

## SPECIALTY OF THE HOUSE

| | | |
|---|---|---|
| HARD SHELL CRABS - (1 ORDER) --- 3.00 --- | 4.00 |
| LOBSTER CRABS (SEASONAL) | 3.00 |
| SMOKED FISH SALAD | 1.25 |

## RAW

| | | |
|---|---|---|
| CLAMS (Cherry Stones) --- (6 ON HALF SHELL) | 1.50 |
| " (Little Necks) ---- (" " " " ) | 1.50 |
| OYSTERS (" " " " ) | 1.50 |

## FROM OUR MODERN OVENS

| | | |
|---|---|---|
| CLAM IMPERIAL (4 TO AN ORDER) | 1.25 |
| CRAB IMPERIAL (3 " " " ) | 1.75 |
| SHRIMP ROLL | .75 |

## COOKED

| | | |
|---|---|---|
| CRAB MEAT DELIGHT COCKTAIL | 3.00 |
| SHRIMP COCKTAIL | 2.50 |
| SHRIMP CREOLE (A BOWL) | 1.25 |
| SAUTEE CRABS (2 TO AN ORDER) | 3.50 |
| " SHRIMP (5 TO AN ORDER) | 3.00 |

## Philadelphia: Center City
## BOOKBINDERS 15TH STREET
### Seafood

**$$**

To clear the record, the 15th Street restaurant is owned by the Bookbinder family, while the Walnut Street Bookbinder's was founded by that family but sold to the Taxin family in the 1940s. Both have similar menus, similarly obliging hours and similarly high standards of quality. Made to choose, I'd have to say honestly that whichever Bookbinder's I'm near gets my patronage. The 15th Street establishment is operated by the fourth generation of the seafood-knowledgeable Bookbinder clan who dish up their specialties at a center-city location convenient to many hotels, theaters and offices. The restaurant's decor, like that of some old established New Orleans restaurants, reminds you that you're here for food, not frills. Feast on the likes of lobster flown in fresh from Maine. Chincoteague oysters, opened with lightning speed, are served chilled, stewed, barbecued or fried and accompanied with chicken salad. On Friday, both Bookbinder restaurants offer excellent bouillabaisse by the cup or plate. There's always thick, rich snapper soup, made unsober with sherry, and, always, a variety of freshly caught fish. Meat-eaters make up a surprisingly large percentage of the clientele, attracted by the restaurant's excellent steaks and chops. Desserts are big portions dished out at reasonable prices. The candied walnut pie is a dandy concoction of fresh apple pie with cream and walnuts. Drinks include a selection of seafood-loving wines, Guinness Stout, imported beer and ale.

BOOKBINDERS 15TH STREET, 215 South 15th Street, Philadelphia. Telephone: (215) 545-1137. Hours: Monday-Friday 11:30 am-11 pm; Saturday to 1 am; Sunday to 10 pm. All major cards. Reservations advised. Full parking service. Nearby parking garages. Children's menu.

## Fresh from the Sea

| | |
|---|---|
| BROILED FRESH RED KING SALMON, Lemon Butter | 11.50 |
| FRIED CANADIAN SILVER SMELTS , Tartar Sauce | 8.50 |
| BROILED FRESH NEW ENGLAND SWORDFISH, Anchovy Butter | 10.75 |
| BROILED FRESH OCEAN BLUEFISH, Maitre d'Hotel | 9.50 |
| BROILED WHOLE JERSEY FLOUNDER | 9.25 |
| BROILED FRESH FILET OF BOSTON SCROD, Butter Sauce | 9.75 |
| GOLDEN FRIED or SAUTED FRESH DEEP SEA SCALLOPS, Tartar Sauce | 9.75 |
| FRESH FILET OF FLOUNDER Stuffed with CRABMEAT (A Gourmet's Delight) | 11.75 |
| STEAMED ALASKA KING CRAB LEGS, Drawn Butter | 12.75 |
| HALF COLD LOBSTER WITH SHRIMP SALAD | 10.25 |

## Maine Lobsters

The Finest Lobsters are LIVE LOBSTERS, rushed by air daily from the cold waters of Maine

| | |
|---|---|
| WHOLE MAINE CHICKEN LOBSTER 1¼ lb. | 12.75 |
| SMALL, 1¾ lb. | 17.95 |
| MEDIUM, 2½ to 2¾ lb. | 22.95 |
| JUMBO, 3 lb. to 3½ lb. | 24.95 |
| LOBSTER COLEMAN ...........................STUFFED WITH CRABMEAT | |
| CHICKEN & SMALL LOBSTER 2.25 Extra          MEDIUM & JUMBO LOBSTER 3.50 Extra | |
| LOBSTER STEW | 12.00 |
| LOBSTER NEWBURG | 13.50 |
| Delicate pieces of Fresh Lobster Blended with a Rich Sauce of Wine, Cream and Butter | |
| LOBSTER THERMIDOR | 14.95 |
| Chunks of Lobster removed from the shell and combined with a tempting sauce of Mushrooms, Green Peppers, Pimentoes, Spices and Wine — then replaced in the shell and baked with Cream Sauce | |

## Bookbinders Specialty

| | |
|---|---|
| BROILED BABY SOUTH AFRICAN LOBSTER TAILS | 14.95 |

A Gourmet's Delight

## Prime Meats and Fowl

| | |
|---|---|
| U. S. PRIME SIRLOIN MINUTE STEAK | 11.50 |
| 12 oz. without bone, of Western Steer Beef, Perfectly aged and artfully broiled to your specifications. | |
| LARGE SIRLOIN STEAK (1 lb.) | 13.00 |
| LAMB CHOPS (2) | 10.50 |
| Thick Tender Chops from carefully selected racks of young spring lamb. | |
| THREE FINGER STEAK (2 lbs.) | 26.00 |
| For Two | |
| U. S. PRIME FILET MIGNON | 13.00 |
| The very tender Heart of Beef with all Savory Juices sealed in. | |
| BROILED CHOPPED SIRLOIN, Onions | 8.00 |
| BROILED HALF SPRING CHICKEN, Disjointed | 7.25 |

# CAFÉ AT BON APPETIT
## Light Lunch $

Although I've seen men lunching here, the man who shared a meal with me at this attractive above-the-cookware-store restaurant was not thrilled. It could have something to do with the flower-and-bird print chintz. Or the preponderance of women patrons. Both may tend to make men feel they've invaded the Women's Exchange. Whatever the reason, what he failed to appreciate, I liked well enough to return for more. Two large skylights keep the place in touch with the weather. Hanging plants add to the feeling of communing with nature. The menu offers a limited but good selection of soups, salads, pâtés and sandwiches. All reflect the seasons as well as the whim of the cook. In summer the soup might be cold Persian cucumber made of dill-seasoned yogurt thick with cucumber and raisins or a tangy cream of sorrel.

CAFÉ AT BON APPETIT, (above Bon Appetit cookware store), 213 South 17th Street, Philadelphia. Telephone: (215) 546-1491. Lunch: Monday-Saturday 11:30-3; closed Sunday. Cards: AE, MC, VISA. Reservations accepted. No bar; but you may bring your own wine. Nearby parking garages.

## Philadelphia: Center City
## CAFÉ LAFITTE
International

**$$**

The tables wear floor-length skirts under their fresh white cloths. Chairs are pink, high-backed and handsome. The walls are covered with a dark-background floral material that looks—and I'm certain is—expensive. If the new Café Lafitte sounds stylish that's because it is. Moreover, under the management of a new chef the place has a menu that lives up to the decor. At a recent dinner tasting, we found a new menu that featured Continental, Creole and even Oriental dishes. Among our samples: potage Le Ruth, based on the Pernod-flavored oyster and artichoke recipe made famous by that New Orleans restaurant, pork enhanced by apples, raisins and pecans, flounder with sherry-spiked hollandaise and a cream puff-based strawberry tart. Lafitte is convenient to theaters and major department stores.

CAFÉ LAFITTE, 1304 Drury Lane, Philadelphia. Telephone: (215) 985-1181. Lunch: Monday-Friday 11:30-2:30. Dinner: Tuesday-Saturday 5:30-10:30. Sunday brunch 1:30-4:30. Cards: AE, DC, MC, VISA. Reservations advised. Full bar service. Nearby parking garages.

## Philadelphia: Manayunk
## CAPT'N Z'S
### Seafood

$$

You never know who will be sitting next to you at Manayunk's Capt'n Z's. It might be a young and handsome Phillies pitcher, the host of a local TV talk show, a couple who live across the river in one of those cost-a-fortune Penn Valley castles or a Manayunk blue-collar neighbor here for a quick beer. You never know and you probably never will. At Z's, the lights are dimmed to the level of a Hernando's Hideaway. People-watching may be discouraged but over-eating isn't. The emphasis is on sea treasures and big portions. Snapper soup arrives in those big, heavy bowls you associate with oatmeal. An order of crabmeat cooked in butter and garlic will bring big crab chunks and enough of them to almost guarantee you'll open your belt a notch. King crab legs, another favorite here, look large enough to take top billing in a monster movie. Accompaniments tend to be pretty mundane. Stewed tomatoes, big French fries, applesauce and cold, rubbery rolls were remembered from a recent visit. Management provides a complimentary glass (eye-cup size) of thin white wine with your meal.

CAPT'N Z'S, Fountain and Umbria Streets, Philadelphia. Telephone: (215) 482-9623. Lunch: Monday-Friday from 11 am. Dinner: Monday-Thursday from 3; Friday and Saturday from 4. No cards. No reservations. Municipal parking nearby.

# Philadelphia: East Philly
# CHEESE CELLAR
## Cheese

$

"If a lady loses her bread cubes in a fondue, she pays with a kiss to the man on her right. If a man loses, he buys the next round of drinks." If that bit of information from the Cheese Cellar's fondue menu sounds like pure Mazola to you, so will the Cellar's intimate booths, candles dripping wax over wine bottles and young lovers holding hands. If you're a pushover for any of the above, you'll probably enjoy the Cheese Cellar as much as I do. Along with the above-mentioned clichés, the Cellar serves some acceptable food and drink at equally acceptable prices. The menu offers soups, salads, fondues for two and a variety of substantial cheese dishes including raclette, grilled sandwiches, quiche, cheeseburgers and cheese and sausage boards. The most expensive items are the shrimp and scallop and beef fondues priced at $5.25 per person. The raclette is a dinner plate filled with creamy, melted cheese, tiny boiled potatoes and a garnish of pickled onions and gherkins. Cheeseburgers arrive on French bread with a choice of cheeses. Cheesecake, predictably, tops the dessert list, but there's also chocolate fondue, fruit and yogurt crêpes, cappuccino l'amour and Black Forest torte for those who crave something sweeter or more spirited.

CHEESE CELLAR, 120 Lombard Street, Philadelphia. Telephone: (215) 923-6112. Hours: Monday-Saturday noon-1 am; Sunday 1 pm-11 pm. All major cards. Reservations accepted. Full bar service. Street parking.

# CENT'ANNI
## Italian
**$$**

There are a lot of good Italian cooks in South Philly and Cent'Anni has two of them. One is the regular chef of this small, cozy restaurant. The other is owner Charlie De Rosa's mother. According to waiter-turned-restaurateur De Rosa, Mom wouldn't trust anyone else with the important task of cooking the "gravy" for her son's two-year-old restaurant. (In South Philly's Italian community, gravy means the wonderful tomato sauce that is the base for many dishes.) The gravy is made fresh daily in Mom's favorite pot. The rest of the cooking she leaves to the Cent'Anni chef. Let me say here that while prices on the Cent'Anni menu are fairly steep, generous portions and obvious quality should justify them to most check payers. Many dishes are large enough to be shared. The special Cent'Anni salad with tuna is one of those. Moreover, it doubles as an antipasto for two. Fettuccine Alfredo is another sharable dish, a heavenly combination of al dente

## APPETIZERS

| | | | |
|---|---|---|---|
| Antipasto | 3.75 | Clams Casino | 3.50 |
| Roast Peppers & Anchovies | 2.75 | Prosciutto Melon (in Season) | 3.25 |
| Mussels (Red or White) | 3.00 | Artichokes | 3.00 |
| Sliced Tomato & Anchovies | 2.75 | Peppers Vesuvio | 3.00 |

## SALADS

| | | | |
|---|---|---|---|
| | | Scungilli Salad | 2.75 |
| Hearts of Lettuce & Tomato | 1.75 | Spec. Cent'Anni Salad (2) | 3.75 |
| Baccala | 2.50 | Tomatoes Napoli | 1.75 |

## PASTAS

| | | | |
|---|---|---|---|
| Tomato Sauce | 5.00 | Oil & Garlic | 5.25 |
| Marinara Sauce | 5.00 | Tuna Fish (Red or White) | 6.25 |
| Scungilli | 6.00 | Clams (Red or White) | 6.25 |
| Mushrooms | 5.75 | Anchovies | 6.00 |
| Butter | 5.00 | Calamari | 6.25 |
| Carbonero | 6.00 | Rigatoni | 5.00 |

ribbons of pasta in an almost embarassingly rich sauce of cheese, butter and cream. Recommended are the veal pic-cante with its buttery lemon sauce and the chicken Gia-como, one of several interesting chicken dishes on the menu. This one combines tender chicken parts, sliced green peppers and mushrooms, whole artichoke hearts, ripe olives and capers. Try it. You should like it. Dessert is compli-mentary and light. We got two small slices of dry seed cake and some fresh apple wedges, just enough after the sub-stantial meal. Cent'Anni's pocket-sized bar serves generous, well-made cocktails and decent, if not rave-worthy, house wine. Other wines are also available. The restaurant has bright red accents and lighting that is extremely flattering to the well-dressed patrons who, on our Friday night visit, were of all ages, from pre-school to post-parenting.

CENT'ANNI, 770 South Seventh Street, Philadelphia. Tele-phone: (215) 925-5558. Lunch: Monday-Friday 11:30-2:30. Dinner: Monday-Thursday 5-11; Friday and Saturday to midnight; Sunday dinner 2-10. No cards. Reservations ac-cepted. Full bar service. Street parking.

## ENTREES

### VEALS

| | |
|---|---|
| Veal Cutlets Milanaise | 9.00 |
| Veal Parmigiana | 9.25 |
| Stuffed w/Spinach ...9.50  Egg Plant 9.50 Peppers & Mushrooms ..9.50 | |
| Veal Scallopini (Red or White) Peppers & Mushrooms....9.50 | |
| Veal Piccanti | 9.50 |
| Veal Francaise | 9.50 |
| Veal Saltimbocca | 9.75 |
| Veal Pizzaioli | 9.50 |
| Veal Marsala | 9.50 |

### CHICKEN

| | | | |
|---|---|---|---|
| Chicken Cacciatore....7.75 | | Giacamo | 8.50 |
| Chicken Spezzantini Alla Cent'Anni 7.75 | | Siciliano | 8.25 |
| Chicken Cutlet Parmigianna..6.75 | VERONA | | 8.25 |
| Stuffed w/Spinach........7.50  Peppers & Mushrooms ...7.53 | | | |

### SEAFOOD

Shrimp Cacciatore 9.50   Shrimp Scampi 9.50
Shrimp Avellino 9.75  Shrimp Parmigiana 9.75  Shrimp Francaise . 9.75

Flounder Francaise 8.00  Flounder Parmigiana 8.00  Flounder Livornese 8.00

**Philadelphia: Center City**
## CLUB RITTENHOUSE
**International** **$$**

This club isn't a club at all. It's a restaurant open to all, but don't let that stop you from pretending you're a card-carrying member of the classy Rittenhouse Square crowd. Club Rittenhouse lets you savor your drink or your carefully prepared meal in quiet, slightly shabby surroundings that won't win space in *Architectural Digest* but would be right at home almost anywhere old money feels comfortable. Delights of the small menu on a recent visit included duck pâté that was dark, robustly delicious. The rest of the duck arrived bedded in wild rice, wearing apricot halves and a handsome and suitably sweet apricot glaze. Veal at the Club is of excellent quality and one of the more interesting dishes using it has a truffled, Madeira-splashed cream sauce. Coffee is freshly ground and expertly brewed. In addition to grinding coffee beans, a caring kitchen staff does meat cutting and baking on the premises.

CLUB RITTENHOUSE, 256 South 20th Street, Philadelphia. Telephone: (215) 732-1990. Lunch: Monday-Friday from 11:30 am. Dinner: daily from 5:30 pm; closed Sunday. Cards: AE, MC, VISA. Reservations advised. Full bar service. Street parking.

## Soups

Potage à la Maison      1.75

Onion Soup Gratinée      2.00

## Hors D'oeuvres

### Shrimp and Beer Batter      3.50
Shrimp, deep fried in a beer batter, and
served with a pungent fruit sauce.

### Stuffed Mushrooms      4.50
Mushroom caps stuffed with scallops, fine herbs and spices.

### Escargot Chablisien      3.50

### Salads of season
Salads will change with the availability
of fresh ingredients.

## Entreés

### Flondre Sautée aux Concombres      6.95
Filet of Flounder sautée with white wine and cucumbers.

### Scallops Coquille aux Champignon      7.95
Sea scallops sautée in butter, white wine, and mushrooms.

### Escallope de Veau      10.25
Nature veal, sautée and served in a cream
sauce of madiera wine and Truffles.

### Rack of Lamb Persilée      11.50
Baby rack of lamb baked with a glaze of
dijon mustard and seasoned breadcrumbs.

### Beef à la Maison
All beef entrées are prime aged.
Featured entrée changes nightly.

### Fowl a la Maison
Featured entrée changes nightly.

## Assorted Desserts

## Philadelphia: Center City
## THE COMMISSARY
International                                    $$

The original Commissary concept was to dish out caviar-class food in a chic, cafeteria setting. Later, for fans of Commissary food who would rather sit than fight the chow line, owner-innovator Steve Poses added a small, full-service dining room upstairs. The Commissary owes its success to convenience as well as its unusual food combinations. Doors open early to pamper the breakfasting broker or secretary with fresh-baked croissants and well-made omelets. After that, there's all-day service on salads, charcuterie and a bevy of daily hot specials. For the upstairs diner, the big blackboard chalks up an even more imaginative menu.

### SOUPS
| | |
|---|---|
| Belgian Vegetable | 2.25 |
| Cold Gazpacho | 2.00 |

### SALADS
| | |
|---|---|
| Mixed Greens | 1.50 |
| Bibb Lettuce with Watercress and Bleu Cheese | 2.75 |
| Zucchini - Mushroom Vinaigrette | 1.75 |
| Tomato - Dill Vinaigrette | 1.50 |
| Boston Lettuce with Toasted Walnuts | 2.25 |

### APPETIZERS
| | |
|---|---|
| Country Pâté | 3.50 |
| Grilled Oysters with Anchovy Butter | 2.50 |
| Batter - Fried Mushrooms with Hollandaise | 2.25 |
| Crab & Scallop Crêpe with Saffron Sauce | 2.75 |
| Grilled Scallops in Mushroom Caps | 2.75 |

### ENTRÉES
| | |
|---|---|
| Poached Rainbow Trout with Bercy Butter & Sautéed Mushrooms | 7.75 |
| Sautéed Sole with Chinese Vegetables | 8.50 |
| Broiled Swordfish with Bercy Butter | 7.75 |
| Crisped Shrimp with Cremona Mustard Sauce | 8.50 |
| Malaysian Pork Saté | 7.25 |
| Broiled Sirloin with Roquefort Butter | 9.75 |
| Shashlik of Lamb with Kasha & Cucumbers | 8.75 |
| Thai Beef Curry with Cashews, Oranges & Snowpeas | 8.25 |
| Sweetbread Fritters | 7.75 |
| Cornish Hen à la Russe with Walnuts & Plum Sauce | 7.25 |
| Turkey Breasts with Almond Coating in Brown Butter | 7.25 |
| Chicken Breasts with Mushrooms, Cream & Brandy | 6.75 |
| Italian Egg Noodles with Sauce Monsumer (shrimp) | 5.50 |

### DESSERTS
The Commissary employs 7 full-time bakers who produce extraordinary desserts

Lunch might start with cold gazpacho then move on to something as exotic as batter-fried sole with bananas or chicken fruit salad with horseradish mayonnaise. Dinner could begin with grilled oysters and anchovy butter, be highlighted by a Thai beef curry with cashews, oranges and snowpeas, then finish with chocolate mousse cake or Sacher torte, both first-rate creations from the Commissary's staff of bakers. If you'd like your dessert later, at home, the cashier will wrap up one of the sweets, a meringue mushroom or chocolate chip cookie perhaps, for take home. The Commissary bar offers a different wine of the day by the glass or bottle. There's also a conventional wine list.

THE COMMISSARY, 1710 Sansom Street, Philadelphia. Telephone: (215) 569-2240. Hours downstairs: Monday-Friday 8 am-11 pm; Saturday 9 am-midnight; Sunday 10:30 am-10 pm. Hours upstairs: Monday-Friday 10:30 am-2:30 pm; Monday-Thursday 5:30 pm-11 pm, Friday and Saturday 5:30 pm-midnight for dinner. Cards: AE, DC, MC, VISA. Reservations accepted upstairs. Full bar service. Nearby parking garages.

## Philadelphia: Center City
## CORNED BEEF ACADEMY
Sandwiches/Breakfast $

For those moments when all you really crave is a great sandwich made with real corned beef, roast beef or turkey, or a variety of freshly made salads, Corned Beef Academy is your kind of place. Good breads, thick fillings and a brisk turnover make the Academy a popular eat-in or take-out spot with the center-city business community.

CORNED BEEF ACADEMY, 121 South 16th Street, Philadelphia. Telephone: (215) 665-0460. Breakfast: Monday-Saturday 7-10 am. Lunch: Monday-Saturday from 11:30 am. No cards. No alcoholic beverages.

# Philadelphia: Center City
# DÉJÀ VU
## French

$$$

Déjà Vu is small, dark and handsome, like its omnipresent owner-chef Sal Montezinos. If it were in Manhattan, it would probably be one of those places where reservations are booked months in advance. It is a restaurant that has been decorated under Montezinos' guidance, and clearly at great expense, in a style that manages, miraculously, to look ornate yet seductive. And the food? At last check, the menu had been pruned of any dish Montezinos didn't feel was uniquely his. The result is a prix fixe meal that for the current rate offers each diner a choice of five first courses (mousse of pike, light goose liver pâté, snails, salad or onion soup), freshly made champagne fruit sorbet, seven entrées, a sweet and coffee. The entrées touch all bases. There's sole fried with hot sauce, filet mignon with green peppercorns, lamb with ginger, sweetbreads with truffles, veal with lemon, chicken with curry and venison with lingonberries. Montezinos is passionately proud of his provisions and proclaims on the menu's first page that all are the best available. Local restaurant critics generally agree. The Déjà Vu wine cellar is one of the few in the area to stock rare vintages as well as some more affordable current offerings. Those with the cash can sip 1929 Château Lafîte Rothschild with the côtelettes or tournedos.

DÉJÀ VU, 1609 Pine Street, Philadelphia. Telephone: (215) 546-1190. Hours: Tuesday-Saturday 6 pm-11 pm. Cards: AE, DC, VISA. Reservations advised. Full bar service. Street parking or nearby lot.

# Menu

### Prix Fixe $27⁵⁰

La Mousseline de Brochet, sauce du Chef
  (mousse of Pike)
or
Le Délice de Foie d'Oie à l'Armagnac
  (goose liver with armagnac)

Les Escargots "Déjà-Vu"
  (snails of the house)

La Mosaïque sur Endives
  (our salad with endive)

Le Gratin d'Oignons au Parfum
  (a delicacy of oignons with Calvados)

Le Sorbet au Champagne et Fruits

Les Goujonnettes de Sole frites "Mer du Nord"
  (fried sole with flot sauce)

Le Tournedos au poivre vert
  (filet mignon with green pepper)

Les Côtelettes d'Agneau farcies "Fleur de Gingembre"
  (lamcutlets with ginger)

La cassolette de Ris de veau "Alan-Antoine"
  (sweetbreads with truffles)

Les filetz mignon de Veau Acidulée
  (veal in lemon extract)

Les Aiguillettes Rosées de Volaille "Indien"
  (chicken breast in curry)

Les Noisettes de Chevreuil "Montez"
  (venaison and lingonberries)

Le Chariot de Douceurs

Café

Chef de cuisine Alan Polet.

## Philadelphia: East Philly
## DIONYSOS
### Greek

**$$**

Despite the city's Greek-derived name, Philadelphia has not proved an especially hospitable host to Greek restaurants. Of several that have struck out in this small Society Hill neighborhood, only Dionysos has survived. The restaurant offers a fairly standard Greek menu in a setting that is restrained—at least until the Greek dancing starts. Food has always been nicely prepared and at nice prices. You can eat your way through taramosalata (the whipped fish-roe appetizer), avgolemono (egg-lemon chicken soup), moussaka (eggplant and lamb layered with béchamel and tomato sauces), baklava (layered pastries dripping sweet syrup) and coffee, all for just over $10. For something special try the spanakotiropita, an unwieldy name for a meltingly tender, hot pastry layered with spinach and cheese, or the hot squid, grilled in olive oil and lemon. Lamb lovers will want to explore the menu's range of offerings. It goes from broiled to roasted to marinated and skewered.

DIONYSOS SUPPER CLUB, 600 South Second Street, Philadelphia. Telephone: (215) 922-4222. Hours: daily 5 pm-2 am. Closed Monday. Cards: AE, DC, MC, VISA. Reservations advised. Full bar service. Street parking.

# ENTREES

**ARNI STAMNAS**   7.25
Baked Spring Lamb with Orzo

**MOUSSAKA**   5.50
A Light and Frothy Combination of Eggplant
Meat and Creamy Bechamel Sauce

**ARNI KAPAMA**   6.75
Greek Baked Spring Lamb Garni
Moussaka, Rice and Vegetables

**ARNI EXOHIKON**   6.75
Baby Spring Lamb Braised with Various Vegetables
Wrapped in Foil

**SATYRIKON**   7.25
Combination of All the Chef's Specialties

**PASTITSIO**   5.50
Baked Macaroni with Ground Meat,
Mediterranean Style (Individual)

**GARIDES TOURKOLIMANO**   6.75
Shrimps Sauteed in Wine and Baked en Casserole
with Feta Cheese, Tomato and Garlic

**ASTAKOS NISSIOTIKOS**   12.00 —
Imported Baby Lobster Tails, Broiled in the
Style of the Greek Island

**PASHA DAVA**   6.75
Eggplant Filled with Tender Lamb Cubes and
Topped with Cheese (Our Chef's Specialty)

**KALAMARAKIA TIGANITA**   6.25
Squid, Grilled in Olive Oil and Lemon

---

# GRILLADES & ROTIS

**BROILED FLOUNDER Stuffed
with CRABMEAT**   7.25
Lemon Butter Sauce

**KEFTEDAKIA SKARAS**   5.50
Mid-Eastern Style Chopped Beef, Lamb
and Parsley Barbecued to Order

**SOUVLAKIA MOSCHARISIA**   11.50
Skewered Filet Mignonettes Marinated in Cognac
and Wine, Served with Mushrooms and Peppers

**ARNI STA KLIMATA**   7.25
Roast Lamb Prepared Country-Style on
Dried Vine-Leaves

**PAIDAKIA**   8.25
Succulent Broiled Spring Lamb Chops

**BEKRI MEZE**   6.00
A Bacchanal of Calf's Liver, Sweetbreads,
Greek Sausage and Greek Cheese in Wine

**SINAGRIDA**   7.50
Broiled, Lemon Sauce

**MOSCHARAKI GALAKTOS**   7.50
Milk-Fed Baby Veal Roast, Garnished with
the Chef's Preparation

**SOUVLAKIA ARNISIA**   7.75
Skewered Lamb Marinated in the Chef's
Special Wine Tomato Herbs and Peppers

**BRISOLA "DIONYSOS"**   10.25
Prime New York Sirloin

**FILETAKIA MIGNON
RIGANATA**   11.50
Sliced Filet Mignon with Oregano Lemon Sauce

**BROILED CALVES LIVER**   7.25
with Onions or Bacon

**BROILED OR FRIED
SWEETBREADS**   7.25
Cooked in Wine Sauce

**FILET MIGNON**   12.00
Prime Filet in a Crepe Prepared with
Madeira Sauce

---

# SALADS

**HORIATIKI "DIONYSOS"**   2.50
Our Special Greek Village Salad

**TOMATO SALAD**   3.50
Greek Dressing and Feta Cheese

---

# CHEESES

**FETA PARNASOU**   2.50    **KASERI**   3.50

# DOWNEY'S
## Irish                                        $$

Downey's is one of those obliging places where, at hours when most restaurant staffs would wave you away, you'll be fed and made to feel welcome. There's food and drink from 11:30 am into the wee hours. Lunch features sandwiches like broiled fillet with sautéed onions, pimientos, mushrooms and melted cheese on a long roll, eggs and the obligatory—for a pub—Irish stew. Most are served with the restaurant's thick, delicious potato pancakes. Dinner provides hearty fare like corned beef and cabbage, Irish stew and stuffed pork chops—all specialties marked on the menu by shamrocks. There's also a selection of somewhat more delicate dishes like flounder Florentine and roast chicken with orange sauce and garnish. Dessert, should you have room for more, should be the Irish whiskey cake dotted with walnuts and topped with real whipped cream. The coffee is freshly ground and excellent. Downey's first floor is divided into a handsome bar, where top sports names have been known to gather to lift a few in celebration, and a dining room with lacquered vintage-newspaper front pages on the walls and crisp, white-lace curtains. It all makes for a pleasant drinking and dining experience and, unless you arrive at an odd hour, for crowds. Don't say you weren't warned.

DOWNEY'S DRINKING HOUSE AND DINING SALOON, Front and South Streets, Philadelphia. Telephone: (215) 629-0526. Lunch: Monday-Friday 11:30-5; Saturday 11:30-4. Dinner: Monday-Friday 5-10:45; Saturday 5-10; Sunday 4-10. Supper: Monday-Friday 11-1; Saturday 11-1:30; Sunday 10-1:30. Sunday brunch 11:30-3. Cards: AE, CB, DC, MC, VISA. Reservations accepted. Full bar service. Street parking.

# Appetizers

**Soup du Jour** ask your Downeyperson ...........................................

    **Fresh Melon** whatever kinds are in season and especially flavorful ............. 1.75

    **Irish Potato Soup** the traditional recipe. rich and thick ... cup ... .75 ...... bowl ... 1.50

**Vegetable Vinaigrette** a garden fresh vegetable steamed aldente with vinaigrette dressing .......... 1.75

**Spinach Salad** with onion, bacon bits, fresh mushrooms, and our Special Downey's Dressing ................. 1.75

**Green Salad** Boston & Romaine with carrot laces, tomato wedges, cucumbers and Special Downey's Dressing ... 1.50

**Meat Tart** silky quiche-like shell with today's special meat-and-herb filling .................... 1.75

**Sausage Roll** sweet sausage wrapped in fluffy bread dough served with mustard and horseradish sauce .......... 1.75

# Dinner

**Shrimp Scampi** shrimp sauteed in our own garlic butter ............................. 8.50

**Flounder Florentine** baked delicate fresh flounder bedded on spinach, covered with our mornay, and accompanied by a boiled potato ..................................... 6.50

**Rack of Lamb** a cluster of the very finest ... a delicate delight complimented by mint jelly ................. 13.50

**Filet Mignon** we import these prime ten ounce prizes all the way from Colorado's Monfort Farms because no other approaches their quality ................................ 11.95

**Sirloin Steak** another Monfort Farms product: 13 ounces of the tenderest, most flavorful sirloin served anywhere 12.95

**Corned Beef and Cabbage** the purist version. A hearty half-pound of prime corned beef, sliced thick, with a quarterhead of fresh steamed cabbage and a boiled potato ......... 9.75

**Irish Stew** a dinner-size crockful of our particularly hearty lamb, onion, and potato stew .................... 4.75

**Stuffed Pork Chop** an old-fashioned herb stuffing between the ribs of a double loin chop. The greatest! .... 8.25

**Roast Duck** Half a Long Island duck done crispy in the classic manner ............................. 8.95

**Steamship** Downey's own steamship round—sliced thin in natural juices ............................. 7.50

**Hamburger Front Street** eight ounces of special ground sirloin with chopped onions and parsley; on a crisp Kaiser roll (Philadelphia Magazine's best) .... 3.95    with hot cheddar cheese .... 4.25

**Orange Chicken** a half-chicken delicately done with mandarin slices. orange sauce and garnishes ......... 5.95

**Veal Downey** sauteed scallops of veal aflame with brandy and covered with cream and mushroom sauce .. 7.95

**Baked Ham** smokehouse ham prepared with cloves, bubblin' brown sugar, and tart pineapple ............. 7.25

**Specials, too.** Ask your Downeyperson.
Appropriate entrees that don't include potatoes are served with the potato pancake
Philadelphia Magazine rated the city's best, hot apple sauce and a special vegetable.

# Desserts & Beverages
All desserts made on premises in Downey's own bakery.

**Irish Whiskey Cake** our pride! A special bundt cake with ground walnuts generously doused with Tullamore Dew, (turned daily during aging), and topped by a mound of real whipped cream .......... 2.00

**Hot Homemade Apple Pie** a traditional treatment of a certain Grandmother's guarded recipe. Garnished with cheddar cheese or whipped cream .................................. 2.00

**Ice Cream** Bassett's French Vanilla or Haagen-Dazs Chocolate Chip, Boysenberry Sherbet, or Irish (naturally) Coffee ................................................. 1.50

**Chocolate Chip Cheese Cake** the richest you've ever tasted. A real graham cracker crust adds its own personality .................................. 2.00

**Bread Pudding** warm traditional bread pudding topped with whipped cream ....................... 1.75

**Berries 'n Cream** Strawberries (or other particularly tasty berries) with cream or whipped cream ............ 2.00

**Special Desserts.** Your Downeyperson will tell you about them.
Coffee .50 · Tea .50 · Sanka .50 · Irish Coffee 2.50 · Iced Tea .75
Iced Irish Coffee 2.50 · Soft Drinks .75 · Downey Mug 1.50

**Shamrock Birthday Cake,** or any other special dessert available on one day's notice.
**We fresh-grind our own special blend of coffee daily.**

## Philadelphia: Center City
## FIDDLER
**Deli**

Those of us who find that restaurants rarely oblige those with offbeat schedules will welcome Fiddler's around-the-clock availability. Arrive mid-morning, mid-afternoon or midnight and you'll be served from the restaurant's big, deli-oriented menu. The three-page folder features juices, soups, salads, sandwiches, hot and cold platters, eggs, dairy dishes, bagels, beverages and even cocktails and beer. If none of the above suits you, maybe you'll find something to please from the printed sheet of new listings that changes daily. During one Fiddler visit, the list gave a choice of 10 platters ranging in price from under $3 for tuna to just under $5 for sautéed veal or baked bluefish. Desserts include a lot of home-baked pastries from the adjoining Fiddler bakery. Fiddler looks like a lot of other fancy downtown dining rooms except that it's a bit more clean-lined, contemporary and larger. It's one of those places where a dine-aloner doesn't feel conspicuous or uncomfortable.

FIDDLER, 1515 Locust Street, Philadelphia. Telephone: (215) 546-7373. Hours: daily from 11 am. Open all night Friday and Saturday. Cards: AE, CB, DC, MC, VISA. No reservations. Full bar service. Garage nearby.

# Philadelphia: Center City
## FRIDAY, SATURDAY, SUNDAY & THURSDAY TOO
### International                                   $$

Friday, Saturday, Sunday once referred to the only three days of the week this tiny, rather urbane restaurant was open for business. That was in the early '70s when Philadelphians were still being told they didn't go out to dinner. When Friday, Saturday, Sunday's management learned that the market for imaginative food served in an offbeat storefront setting was booming, they began expanding the hours. Business is so good now you can dine here seven days a week. The attractions remain Julia Child-generation home-cooking and a good Rittenhouse Square-area address that lets you rub elbows (literally at times, thanks to close quarters) with that area's arty as well as affluent residents. The menu is chalked on slate and offers Italian osso buco, Indian duck curry, lots of French soups, salads and entrées, and some of the best desserts in town. The restaurant opened sans liquor license but now has the proper document for dispensing cocktails and a limited selection of wines.

FRIDAY, SATURDAY, SUNDAY & THURSDAY TOO, 261 South 21st Street, Philadelphia. Telephone: (215) 546-4232. Hours: Monday-Saturday 5:30 pm-10:30 pm, Sunday 5 pm-9:30 pm. Cards: AE, MC, VISA. No reservations. Street parking.

## Philadelphia: Center City
## FISH MARKET
Seafood

**$$**

Philadelphians love seafood enough to support several excellent restaurants featuring it. Those restaurants are for the most part, however, brisk, businesslike spots where the offerings are fresh but unfancy. It took the Fish Market with its chic, butcher block and neon decor and its equally "now" menu to prove Philadelphians have an appetite for seafood that goes beyond snapper soup and fried oysters with chicken salad (an odd combination that is a fading local specialty). The Fish Market will serve you oysters or clams on the half shell but they can also dish up a snappy local bouillabaisse, sole Oscar (with sautéed fish, fresh asparagus, lobster and creamy cheese sauce), swordfish grilled with melted cheese and trout sautéed with bananas and almonds. Desserts are of the heavenly, wholesome variety, including Haagen Däzs ice cream, carrot cake and apple pie so delicious local food writers are regularly asked to pry the recipe from the Fish Market baker. The restaurant has an extensive lunch menu and an excellent bar. For those who'd rather cook it themselves, there's a retail fish market.

FISH MARKET, 124 South 18th Street, Philadelphia. Telephone: (215) 567-3559. Lunch: Monday-Saturday 11:30-4. Dinner: Sunday-Thursday 4-10; Friday and Saturday 4-11. Cards: AE, DC, MC, VISA. Reservations advised. Full bar service. Nearby parking garages.

# ENTREES

**PHILADELPHIAS BEST BOUILLABAISSE**    15⁷⁵

THIS MAGNIFICENT CLASSIC STEW OF THE SEA IS PREPARED HERE OVER A PERIOD OF SIX HOURS. AFTER MAKING THE RICH FISH STOCK, SUCH DELITE'S AS PLUM TOMATOES, LEEKS, PARSLEY, GARLIC, SPICES, AND SAFFRON CREATE THE DELICATELY FLAVORED SAUCE. WE SERVE THE CROCK OF BOUILLABAISSE REPLETE WITH LOBSTER FROM MAINE, SHRIMP, MUSSELS, CLAMS, AND ROCK FISH, WITH GARLIC TOAST.

**SOLE OSCAR**    THE FISH MARKET'S MOST FAMOUS    11⁵⁰
ENTREE IS SAUTEED WITH FRESH ASPARAGUS, CHUNKY LOBSTER MEAT, A SPECIAL JARLSBURG SAUCE

**FRESH JUMBO LUMP CRABMEAT**    SAUTEED    15⁹⁵
WITH SHALLOTS, MUSHROOMS, AND WHITE WINE

**FRESH GRILLED NANTUCKET SWORDFISH**    9⁹⁵
WITH MELTED CHEESE, AND SAUTEED ONIONS

**FRESH FILET OF SOLE**    BAKED WITH ARTICHOKES,    9⁵⁰
SPINACH, MUSHROOMS, AND CHEESE STUFFING

**GENUINE MAINE LOBSTER**    FROM OUR SALT WATER    15⁹⁵
TANK, STEAMED, THEN STUFFED WITH A SPECIAL CRAB ROUX, AND FINISHED TO A GOLDEN BROWN

**FRESH CALICO BAY SCALLOPS**    BAKED IN A    11⁵⁰
SHELL WITH A HAZEL NUT BUTTER

**SCAMPI**    JUMBO PANAMA SHRIMP SAUTEED    12⁵⁰
IN WHITE WINE WITH BAY SCALLOPS

**FRESH BLUE FISH NICOISE**    BAKED WITH TOMATO,    8⁵⁰
ANCHOVIES, CAPERS, AND A SPECIAL SAUCE

**FRESH FILET OF TROUT SICILIAN,** SAUTEED WITH    8⁶⁰
MUSHROOMS, PEPPERS, ONIONS, and WHITE WINE

**GENUINE SOUTH AFRICAN LOBSTER TAIL**    14⁹⁵
BAKED WITH OUR SPECIAL STUFFING

**IDAHO RAINBOW TROUT**    SAUTEED WITH BANANA'S    8⁹⁵
SLICED ALMONDS AND WHITE WINE

**THE FISH MARKET BAKED CRAB**    JUMBO LUMP CRAB    11⁵⁰
BAKED IN A SHELL WITH HERBS, PEPPER, PIMENTO, AND CHEESE

**SHRIMP**    FROM PANAMA DEEP FRIED TO A GOLDEN CRISP    9⁵⁰

———————◆———————

**LOBSTER FRA DIAVOLO**    GENUINE MAINE LOBSTER    15⁹⁵
SAUTEED IN A SPICY TOMATO SAUCE WITH SCALLOPS MUSSELS AND CLAMS

## Philadelphia: Center City
## FROG
## International $$

Talk of Philadelphia culinary trend-setters and Steve
Poses' name is certain to be mentioned. The Frog is Poses'
first restaurant, an exciting, experimental storefront that
has been keeping its competition hopping since it opened in
1973. Decor is as bright and cheery as a pond packed with
water lilies. Green-topped tables look even greener against
white, white walls. Live bouquets bloom on the tables.
Potted plants fill what used to be the store's display window and what is now the back of the Frog bar. Furnishings
include old church pews and mismatched but comfortable
wooden chairs plus a treasure trove of Victorian mirrors,
shelves and cabinet pieces. Menus are chalked on unwieldy
slates. The staff squawks and the customers squint or crane
their necks, but the device helps the kitchen stay in touch
with the seasons. Some of the menu's variety comes from
an early Thai chef, but most of it can be attributed to
Poses, who admits to an eclectic culinary bent. Roast chick-
en boasts almond, apple and apricot bread stuffing and a
Madeira sauce. Lamb curry is served with eggplant and
pecans. Sole might arrive stuffed with smoked salmon and
splashed with a faintly curried cream sauce. Vegetables and
salads also rate lots of attention from the kitchen but then
everything does here. Desserts are a sweet-toother's dream.
The carrot cake, Sacher torte and chocolate mousse cake
are all famous about town. The Frog has one of the city's
more attractive wine lists with an excellent representation
of the better Californian vineyards.

FROG, 264 South 16th Street, Philadelphia. Telephone:
(215) 735-8882. Lunch: Monday-Friday 12-2. Dinner:
Monday-Thursday 6-10; Friday and Saturday 6-11; Sunday
5:30-9:30. Sunday brunch 11:30-2. Cards: AE, DC, MC,
VISA. Reservations advised. Full bar service. Street parking
or nearby lots.

# FROG

264 south 16th street
philadelphia, pa. 19102
pe5·8882

## DINNER MENU SUGGESTIONS *

### • SOUPS •

| | |
|---|---|
| Onion Soup Gratinée | 2·25 |
| Cold Strawberry | 2·25 |
| Cream of Mushroom | 2·00 |

### • SALADS •

Green Salad    1·50                                        Caesar    2·00
FROG Mixed Salad with Romaine, Broccoli, Tomatoes, Olives, &    2·25
Pineapple, Escarole and Walnuts · Rum Vinaigrette    Croutons    2·50
Spinach, Mushroom & Bacon with Roquefort Dressing    2·15

### • APPETIZERS •

| | |
|---|---|
| Ricotta-stuffed Eggplant · Tomato Sauce | 2·15 |
| Pasta with Bay Scallops · Champagne Sauce | 3·50 |
| Three Noodle Appetizer | 2·15 |
| Mussels with Mustard Mayonnaise | 2·25 |
| Deep-fried Spring Rolls | 2·15 |
| Crêpe Jardinière · Artichokes, Tomatoes & Green Peppers | 2·25 |

### • ENTRÉES •

Roast Chicken · Apple, Almond, Apricot Bread Stuffing  Madeira Sauce  8·25
Duck with Orange Sauce    9·25
Medallions of Pork with Peaches, Brandy and Cream    8·50
Veal Piccante    9·25
Sirloin Steak with Herb Butter    10·50
Siamese Chicken Curry with Broccoli and Peanuts    8·25
Oriental Lamb Curry with Eggplant and Pecans    8·15
Shrimp with Soy, Ginger, Garlic and Lemon    8·15
Seafood Stew with Mussels, Shrimp, Scallops & Tomatoes    9·50
Broiled Swordfish with Bearnaise    9·50
Broiled Bluefish with Watercress Butter    8·25
Sole Stuffed with Smoked Salmon · Curried Cream Sauce    8·15

### • DESSERTS •

| | | | |
|---|---|---|---|
| Sacher Torte | 2·50 | Lemon Soufflé | 2·00 |
| Chocolate Mousse Cake | 2·50 | Fruit Tart | 2·50 |
| Cheesecake | 2·25 | Seasonal Fresh Fruit | 2·50 |
| Carrot Cake | 2·25 | Strawberry Crêpe | 2·50 |
| Pecan Pie | 2·25 | | |

*OUR MENUS ARE ON BLACKBOARDS AND FREQUENTLY CHANGE DUE TO SEASONAL AND MARKET AVAILABILITY.

# Philadelphia: Center City
# THE GARDEN
## International $$

Fans of the Garden claim that you could dine here every day of the week and never become bored or disappointed. One look at the Garden's award-winning menu shows that you could dine daily without repeating more than a salad or vegetable. On a chilly evening, dinner might begin with creamy, wonderfully thick and extravagant clam chowder or fettuccine Alfredo, include the Garden's special roast chicken with mushroom purée filling and, for dessert, chocolate mousse. A lighter meal in the garden (for which the place is named) might start with carpaccio Toscana, paper-thin slices of raw beef in a caper sauce that is a specialty of northern Italy, move on to the catch of the day, baked in a parchment that seals in flavors and dill perfume, and wind up with a profiterole packed with ice cream then flourished with fudge sauce. Lunch has its own delights, including slices of glazed baked ham with French mustard and warm, French-style (sans mayonnaise) potato salad, and the Garden's chunky chicken and walnut salad (*with* homemade mayonnaise). The Garden's bar offers an interesting selection of aperitifs, including the currently fashionable Bocuse creation of white wine splashed with framboise. Wines range from some of the most interesting California wines available to $50 bottles of French vintage Champagne. There's even a selection of imported beer. In addition to the handsome main dining room, the Garden boasts a clubby front room known as the oyster bar and a quiet—by center-city standards—garden with umbrella-topped tables that's wildly popular in warm weather.

THE GARDEN, 1617 Spruce Street, Philadelphia. Telephone: (215) 546-4455. Hours: Monday-Saturday 11:30-2:30; 5:30-9:30. Closed Sunday. Cards: AE, MC, VISA. Reservations advised. Full bar service. Reduced fee parking at Latimer garage after 6 pm.

## Appetizers

**½ DOZ. CHINCOTEAGUE OYSTERS ON THE HALF SHELL**
*Opened to order (in season)*

**½ DOZ. CHERRYSTONE CLAMS ON THE HALF SHELL**   2.25
*Small, sweet, succulent, and tender.*

**SMOKED SCOTCH SALMON** 3.95
*"21" brand, rosy, thinly sliced, with capers and pure imported olive oil.*

**CURRIED MUSSELS IN HALF AVOCADO**   2.95
*Cold in a light curry mayonnaise.*

**BAKED CLAMS**   2.95
*On the half shell with an aromatic herb buttered crumb topping.*

**STEAMED MUSSELS**   3.95
*Garlicky, plump, accented with red pepper.*

**CARPACCIO TOSCANA**   3.50
*Sliced raw filet mignon with a lively, spicy, caper sauce.*

**PATE BONNE FEMME**   2.75
*Chicken livers, pork, veal and green peppercorns.*

**PROSCIUTTO AND MELON**   3.50
*Melon with the best Italian ham.*

**WATERCRESS SOUP**   1.75
*Potatoes, leeks and fresh watercress.*

**CLAM CHOWDER**   1.75
*Rich, creamy and filled with chopped clams.*

**ONION SOUP**   1.50
*Golden, winey, full-flavored, crowned with a buttery cheese crouton.*

**FETTUCINE ALFREDO**   3.95
*The classic delightful Roman specialty.*

## Dinner

**STEAK AU POIVRE OR STEAK ROQUEFORT**   10.95
*8 oz. filet mignon, sauteed and flamed in cognac and cream, baked potato.*

**CALVES LIVER**   7.95
*Thinly sliced, lightly sauteed, served with baked potato or pommes frites.*

**CHICKEN BREASTS WITH CEPES**   8.95
*Breast of chicken, imported mushrooms and prosciutto in a sauce with cognac and cream.*

**ELEGANT RACK OF LAMB (3 Chops)**   9.95
*Seasoned with garlic and herbs, served with linguine or baked potato.*

**ONE HALF ROAST DUCKLING A L'ORANGE**   9.75
*Served with an orange and green peppercorn sauce, with wild rice.*

**VEAL PICANTE**   8.95
*Thin veal scallops sharpened with lemon and parsley, baked rice parmesan.*

**STEAK TARTARE**   7.95
*Specially ground to your order. Mixed with capers and anchovies, served with spinach and mushroom salad.*

**ROAST CHICKEN THE GARDEN**   7.95
*A small fresh chicken, flamed in cognac, filled with mushroom puree and carved for you—a specialty of our restaurant.*

**PASTA PRIMAVERA**   6.95
*Imported linguine with fresh vegetables in light creamy cheese sauce.*

**BOUILLABAISSE — the special fish soup of Provence**   9.50
*Shrimp, scallops, mussels and bass in a light fish stock, crouton and aioli.*

**THE CHEF'S SPECIALTY**   8.50
*Bebe flounder braised in lettuce with a walnut and mushroom duxelle, sauced with beurre blanc, baked potato.*

**CURRIED SEAFOOD**   8.95
*Shrimps, scallops and mussels in a light curry sauce, with toasted almonds and homemade apricot chutney.*

**SCALLOPS PROVENCAL**   7.95
*Sauteed sea scallops and quartered mushrooms served with rice and herbed tomatoes.*

**MUSSELS AND LINGUINE**   7.95
*Mussels on a bed of linguine seasoned with garlic, white wine, lemon and herbs.*

**CATCH OF THE DAY EN PAPILLOTE**
*Baked in parchment with dill and white wine, served with hollandaise sauce and cucumber salad.*

**LOBSTER CREPE**   7.95
*A crepe filled with shrimp, scallops and mushrooms, sauced with a brandy lobster bisque.*

41

# Philadelphia: Center City
## H. A. WINSTON & CO.
### American
$

Hamburgers in a choice of sizes (seven and 12 ounces) with a choice of some 20 different toppings (from mushroom, pepper and onion to sour cream and caviar) are the focus of this popular local chain. If you're not big on burgers, the Winston people oblige with omelets, sandwiches, soups, salads and even hot platters of ribs, fried chicken or shrimp. Beer is available by the pitcher as well as by the bottle or mug. Modest wines are dispensed by glass or carafe. Cocktails come in five sizes. A Bloody Mary, for example, sells for $1.65 as a drink, $2.75 for a small pitcher and $4.75 and $8.50 for larger pitchers (the last is suitable for a small crowd). At your request, they'll even make your sweet cocktail with artificial sweetener to conserve a few calories. In addition to all of the above, the restaurant pleases its largely youthful clientele with a cart of free condiments, reasonable prices and a cluttered-cozy Tiffany-lamp decor.

H. A. WINSTON & CO., locations at 15th and Locust Streets, Philadelphia, and throughout the Philadelphia area. Telephone: at 15th and Locust, (215) 546-7232. Hours: Monday and Tuesday 11:30 am-11:30 pm; Wednesday and Thursday to midnight; Friday and Saturday to 12:45 am; Sunday 1 pm-11:30 pm. Cards: AE, DC, MC, VISA. No reservations. Full bar service. Adjoining garage.

## Luncheon Special

CROCK OF ONION SOUP
TOSSED SALAD
GLASS OF WINE or MUG OF BEER
Or Choice of Non-Alcoholic Beverage
2.75
Sorry No Substitutes / Served To 4pm Daily

## Dinner Special

CROCK OF ONION SOUP
7oz GOURMETBERGER of Your Choice
GLASS OF WINE or MUG OF BEER
Or Choice of Non-Alcoholic Beverage
4.75
Sorry No Substitutes / Served From 4pm Daily

## Fresh Handcrafted Salads

**THE CHEF'S SALAD BOWL**
Julienne Ham, Turkey Breast, Swiss
Cheese, American Cheese, Bacon &
Egg on a Bed of God's Gorgeous
Greens & Tomato ........................ 3.75
**TUNA SALAD PLATTER** · White Meat
Tuna Salad, Garden Garnishes ....... 3.45

**WAIST WATCHER** · Cottage Cheese,
Egg, Choice of Cheese, Lettuce,
Tomato & Cucumber ..................... 2.45

**DIET BOWL** · Swiss & Muenster Cheese,
Fresh Tuna, Egg & Tomato, topping a
bowl of Garden Green Goodnesses. 3.25

## A La La Carte

**PRIME BEEF RIBS**
Succulently Barbecued ................. 3.95
**CHICKEN LEGS** · 3 Plump "Pulkas"
Winston Fried ............................. 2.95
**SURF & FARM** · Fried Chicken
Breast & Fried Shrimp ................. 5.45

**CHICKEN BREAST** · Boneless and
Juicy · Winston Fried .................... 3.95
**EGGS**
3 with Ham or Bacon ................... 2.95
**SIRLOIN STEAK**
10oz Choice New York Strip ........ 5.95

The Above Served with Vegetable of the Day, Winston Potatoes & Garnish

## Seafood Delights

**FRESH FILLET OF FLOUNDER**
Golden Fried ............................... 3.95
Butter Broiled ............................. 4.45

**TENDER SCALLOPS**
Golden Fried ............................... 4.25
Sauteed .................................... 4.75

**LARGE SHRIMP**
Barbecued ................................. 5.75
Golden Fried .............................. 5.75
**THE SEA COMBO** · Winston Fried
Shrimp, Scallops, Flounder .......... 5.45
**SALMON STEAK**
Butter Broiled ............................ 3.95

The Above Served with Vegetable of the Day, Winston Potatoes & Cole Slaw

## Italian Specialties

**VEAL PARMEGIANA** ................. 5.35
**CHICKEN BREAST PARMEGIANA** 4.75
Both Served with Spaghetti,
Meat Sauce & Garlic Bread

**SPAGHETTI BOWL & Garlic Bread**
Homemade Meat Sauce or Marinara 2.25
**CHEESE RAVIOLI & Garlic Bread**
Homemade Meat Sauce or Marinara 2.50

## SIDE ORDERS

BOWL OF TANGY CHILI ............... 1.95
WINSTON POTATOES .................... .50
CORN BREAD ............................... .25
GARLIC BREAD ............................ .50

TOSSED SALAD ............................ .95
LETTUCE WEDGE & TOMATO ...... .95
SPAGHETTI
Marinara or Homemade Meat Sauce 1.25

AN ONION ORGY · An end to all your onion fantasies ... 1.25

## Desserts

NEW YORK CHEESE CAKE / 1.00
Cherry, Blueberry or Strawberry Topping / .35
HOME MADE PUDDINGS / .65

## Philadelphia: Chinatown
## HO SAI GAI
### Chinese

$

Ho Sai Gai is an immensely popular Chinatown restaurant with a reputation for food that's a shade more adventurous than what is offered by some of its neighbors. It is multi-regional. Soups, for example, include Szechwan (hot and sour or pork and turnip), Mandarin (bean cake with vegetable), Taiwanese (bean cake with pork and sour cabbage), Fu-Kien (fish ball with mushroom) or Peking (minced beef with egg drop.) A shredded pork dish, described as "strange taste," is less strange than it is alternately sweet, sour, hot and spicy. Its flavor secrets include preserved turnips and mustard greens. Vegetarians will enjoy the selection of stir-fried vegetable combinations as well as bean curd, fried-rice noodles and spicy egg noodles. The restaurant decor is decidedly undecorative but no one seems to notice or mind.

HO SAI GAI, 1000 Race Street, Philadelphia. Telephone: (215) 922-5883. Hours: Monday-Friday 11 am-3 am; Friday and Saturday to 4 am. Cards: DC. Nearby parking garage.

The parlor of the Union League Club

# Philadelphia: Chinatown
# IMPERIAL INN
## Chinese                                          $

Philadelphia's Chinatown has been booming in recent years. New restaurants have sprung up, seemingly overnight, like exotic mushrooms. Unfortunately, like mushrooms, many were excellent one day, barely acceptable the next, as chefs took advantage of good reviews to bargain for higher wages elsewhere. An exception is the Imperial Inn, a restaurant that has been reviewed regularly over a period of several years and has always emerged with its first-class rating intact. The Imperial's menu samples the major schools of Chinese cuisine, offering Szechwan, Mandarin, Hunan and Shanghai specialties. Those thrifty column A and B lunches and dinners are also available. The hot and sour soup is one of the best in town. It is hot and it is sour and it is filled with crunchy, chewy, flavorful ingredients like lily buds and cloud ear fungus. Another good choice, steamed clams in garlic sauce, makes a marvelous mess as you dig the clams from their fragrant sauce-splashed shells. Szechwan shrimp, sizzled with garlic, ginger and hot pepper sauce, like all dishes featured from this region, may be ordered with spicing to suit your palate. The restaurant's bar serves small but well-made cocktails. Good lighting and crisp table linens add to the enjoyment of dining here without adding appreciably to the check.

IMPERIAL INN, 941 Race Street, Philadelphia. Telephone: (215) 925-2485. Hours: Monday-Saturday 11:30 am-1 am; Sunday noon-2 am. Cards: AE. Reservations accepted. Full bar service. Garage nearby.

## Kung Pao Chicken                                    4.25

A well known spicy mandarin dish, originated
from the Ching Dynasty. Its main ingredients
are simple: Diced cut of chicken breast, cashew
nut and hot pepper. But, My, What a Taste.

## Imperial Steak Kew                                  5.95

Tender cubes of beef fried with snow peas,
waterchestnuts and bamboo shoots, slices of
Chinese mushrooms in an exotic soya sauce.

## Mandarin Steak Filets (5)                           5.95

Five tender small steaks marinated with our
chef's secret sauce. garnished with preserved
pineapple and cherries. A mingling flavor of
sweet, sour and spicy.

## Cheng-Ban Beef                                      4.95

Diced cut of beef, green pepper and preserved
turnip, cooked in a Mandarin manner and flavored with a mashed bean sauce. A spicy dish.

## Lemon Chicken                                       5.00

Boneless breast chicken, lightly crusted in egg
batter and sauteed. Served in a mild lemon
sauce, topped with crushed almonds.

## Phoenix Chicken                                     5.25

Pressed boneless chicken meat with slices of
ham, lightly breaded and fried to a golden
brown. Garnished with lychees.

## Shrimps, Szechuan Style                             5.25

A very spicy dish. For those who like it hot!
Cooked in real hot pepper sauce, flavored with
garlic and ginger.

## Pa-Chen Duck                                        8.25

An authentic Chinese favorite. Half boneless
braised duck, crowned with a succulent combination of fresh shrimps, squid, slices of ham.
Bar-B-Q pork, shrimp balls, mushrooms, snow
peapods and hearts of Chinese green vegetable.

## Lychee Duck                                         5.75

Chinese barbecued duck to crisp brown, blended with sweet and pungent sauce, subtly flavored with lichees.

# IN SEASON
## International                                    $$

In Season customers don't need a calendar to know the time of year. If there are lots of cold platters of fresh fish, fruit desserts and local vegetables on the menu it must be summer. Fall is signaled by turkey sautéed in vermouth with oysters and local mushrooms, veal steak with artichokes and tomatoes, loin of pork with prunes, apples and cranberry Cumberland sauce. Presentation is an important part of the package, too. An early summer visit found broccoli cooked to keep its green glow, tomato and cucumber garnishes fanned around slices of rare roast beef and German potato salad and brandied cheesecake artistically jeweled with blueberries. The young proprietors say their goal is to offer foods that are visually exciting, nutritionally sound and affordable. The popularity of this small, highly personal restaurant indicates that they have met this goal. Baking is done on the premises and desserts like the restaurant's superb cream cheesecake are a specialty. (The owners justify desserts by calling them foods good for your mental health.)

IN SEASON, 315 South 13th Street, Philadelphia. Telephone: (215) 545-5115. Lunch: Monday-Friday 11:30-2:30. Dinner: Monday-Saturday 6-11; Sunday 5:30-9. Sunday brunch 11:30-2:30. Cards: MC, VISA. Reservations advised. Full bar service. Street parking.

spring vegetable soup — 1.75

mussel soup — 1.75

mushrooms with watercress sauce, curried olives and
eggplant caviar — 2.00

shad roe paté — 3.00

avocado stuffed with scallops and mussels — 3.25

artichoke with bleu cheese vinaigrette — 2.50

Escabeche with avocado and spring vegetables — 4.75

Vegetable Salad In Season — 3.75

Fruit Salad In Season — 4.00

California Seafood Stew — 6.75

Whole Fish broiled with bacon and fresh herbs — 6.00

Chicken Breast with proscuitto in crab sauce — 7.25

Lamb Stew with spring vegetables and fresh dill — 7.00

Calves' Liver sautéed with mustard and brandy — 6.50

Leg of Veal stuffed with spinach, served with cucumber sauce — 8.50

Boneless Strip Steak with cracked peppercorns — 10.00

### Philadelphia: West Philadelphia
### JAPAN HOUSE
Japanese $

Japan House is a campus restaurant in the traditional mode: low-rent basement setting, low-cost food, wine only if you bring your own. The food has that good-for-you look and tastes authentic. Dinners include a seaweed-flavored miso and salad. The generous portions of tempura are great for filling the famished undergrad without emptying his or her wallet. Tempuras range from mixed seafood to vegetarian, all lightly coated with batter and gently fried. There are also a number of vegetarian soups like bean, pea and lentil combinations. For dessert there's a chilled, gelatinous fruit-flavored sweet called kanten that I'm convinced is designed to wean kids off sweets.

JAPAN HOUSE, 4002 Spruce Street, Philadelphia. Telephone: (215) 382-8401. Lunch: Tuesday-Friday 11:30-2:30. Dinner: Tuesday-Thursday 5:30-10; Friday to 10:30; Sunday to 9:30. Closed Monday. Cards: AE, DC, MC, VISA. No reservations. No alcoholic beverages; you may bring your own wine. Street parking.

## Philadelphia: East Philly
## JUDY'S CAFÉ
### International $$

The architectural face that Judy's presents to the world is, in a word, homely. The place looks for all the world like a neighborhood corner taproom out of *Rocky*. Yet behind this ugly duckling facade there's a neat and tidy restaurant with friendly vibes and food prepared with care. Enter through the bar and go beyond to a pink and green dining room with high-gloss wood floors and stamped-tin walls and ceiling. Your tablecloth may be faded and the napkins paper, but the flowers will be fresh and perky. Your waiter or waitress will be dressed as casually as your neighbors at the next table. Well-worn jogging shoes and shapeless jeans were popular on a recent visit. The kitchen is marvelously inventive. Some of the culinary delights are calves liver sautéed with lemon and shallots, flounder nicoise, sautéed shrimp with tarragon, garlic and cream, honey-glazed Cornish hens stuffed with oranges, apples and onions, and watercress-stuffed chicken breast cooked in parchment and served with a good hollandaise. Judy's stays in touch with its less affluent admirers by offering a big meal-in-a-bowl which they call the neighborhood dinner salad. The mixture of Romaine and bibb lettuce contains an assortment of lightly cooked and raw vegetables, sesame seeds and grated Swiss cheese. It sells for $3.50. The restaurant's coffee is excellent and refills are offered. The wine list is small but interesting.

JUDY'S CAFÉ, Third and Bainbridge Streets, Philadelphia. Telephone: (215) 928-1969. Hours: dinner daily from 5 pm. Cards: AE, MC, VISA. No reservations. Full bar service. Street parking.

## Philadelphia: East Philly
## KNAVE OF HEARTS
International

**$$**

Take one run-down but upwardly mobile neighborhood, find an empty store in that neighborhood and make the interior sparkle with paint and imagination. Collect tables and chairs from second-hand furniture stores; collect china, flatware and glasses from flea markets and thrift shops. Avoid, at all costs, perfect match-ups of patterns for table settings. Fill the store window with a jungle of greenery. Now concoct a menu that mixes flavors as imaginatively as an artist mixes colors. Cook the dishes as though you were doing it for good friends. You've just found the formula for a successful storefront restaurant—a restaurant just like Knave of Hearts. Maxfield Parish illustrations of the kingdom of hearts give the restaurant its decorative focal point as well as its name. Reasonable prices and consistently interesting food keep customers coming back for more. Knave's menu runs the gamut from homespun lasagne to exotic chicken coco loco, veal Violette and serpentine

| | |
|---|---|
| The Knave Salad | 1.95 |
| Caesar Salad | 2.50 |
| Salad Yom | 2.95 |
| Greek Salad Bihari | 3.25 |
| Maxfield's Blue Cheese | 2.95 |
| Stuffed Cucumber & Crabmeat Salad | 3.95 |
| Roast Duckling Mont-Morency | 7.95 |
| Filet Mignon Béarnaise 8oz. | 8.95 |
| Serpentine Shrimp | 7.95 |
| Coquilles St. Jacques | 7.95 |
| Knave's Bouillabaise ♥♥♥♥ | 8.95 |
| Veal Violetta | 7.95 |
| Chicken Coco-Loco | 6.95 |
| Decadent Dinner Salad | 4.95 |
| Homemade Lasagna | 4.95 |

shrimp to a conventional French duckling Montmorency. There is always an excellent assortment of salads including a Caesar salad for one, Greek salad and the whopper that Knave describes as its "decadent dinner salad."

KNAVE OF HEARTS, 230 South Street, Philadelphia. Telephone: (215) 922-3956. Lunch: Saturday 12-4. Dinner: Monday-Thursday 6-11; Friday and Saturday to midnight; Sunday 5-10. Sunday brunch 12-4. Cards: AE, DC. Reservations advised. No bar; wine service charge $1 bottle. Street parking.

## Philadelphia: East Philly
# KANPAI
## Japanese                                    $

Big eaters be forewarned. A Kanpai meal is designed to fill the senses rather than the belly. The setting here is splendid with great expanses of glass overlooking graveled Japanese mini-gardens and the decks and shops of the New Market complex. Arrive on a day when business is slow and you may find yourself with your very own teppanyaki chef. Happen in when the place is hopping and you'll be expected to share your black-hatted cook's attention with six tablemates as he chops, flips, flattens, splashes and sizzles your order on his hot, slick metal griddle. Each meal comes with soup, entrée, vegetables, rice and green tea. Entrée choices include steak, shrimp and chicken. The soup is low-calorie onion. Some bean sprouts, sliced vegetables and a small bowl of rice, plus two gingery sauces, send you on your way feeling trim, virtuous and aesthetically sated.

KANPAI, New Market at Head House Square, Philadelphia. Telephone: (215) 925-1532. Lunch: Monday-Friday 11:30-2:30. Dinner: Monday-Friday 5-10:30; Saturday to 11 pm; Sunday 4-9. Cards: AE, DC. Reservations accepted. Full bar service. Underground parking.

# Philadelphia: Center City
## LA CAMARGUE
French

$$$

A meal at La Camargue is an escape to that mysterious region in southern France where gypsies and wild horses are part of the romantic atmosphere. The restaurant was created from one of the original owners' remembrances of years of living in the Camargue. It is white walled, fresh-flower lavished, handsome and lighted so skillfully and softly you just know you've never looked better across a table. La Camargue is now owned by Chef Marcel Brossard, also French, who has a talent for concocting subtle dishes as well as the more assertive specialties of Provence and the Mediterranean. Brossard's hors d'oeuvre include a variety of pâtés, from coarse and spicy terrine de campagne to ultra-fine Strasbourg goose liver paste. For the big spender, there is also beluga caviar. My own favorite beginning for a meal is the soupe de poisson, a rich and satiny, salmon-colored soup into which a fragrant, garlic-pepper paste is stirred at the last minute. If you're budget minded, consider the daily La Camargue lunch special, a hearty-eater's delight that gives a different substantial dish each day (osso buco is one, poulet chasseur another), plus soup or salad and coffee for well under $10. La Camargue's small, cozy bar makes arriving in advance of your reservation an attractive idea. Or drop in after a performance at one of the nearby theaters.

LA CAMARGUE, 1119 Walnut Street, Philadelphia. Telephone: (215) 922-3148. Lunch: Monday-Friday 12-2. Dinner: Monday-Saturday 5:30-11. Closed Sunday. Cards: AE, House, VISA. Reservations advised. Full bar service. Nearby parking garages and lots.

# Menu Gastronomique

## at $ 28⁰⁰

Le Saumon Fumé d'Écosse

La Soupe de Poisson "Cornargue"

Les Serrines Assorties

Le Gratin de
Queues de Langouste

La Darne de
Saumon Béarnaise

La Côte d'Agneau Maréchale

Le Tournedos Trois Sauces

Le Pigeonneau aux Chanterelles

Les Fromages

La Charrette de Desserts Café

## Philadelphia: Center City
## LA DIET
## Low Calorie

**$**

Like eating a banana split while wearing your new skin-tight jeans, finding a seat at La Diet used to be a tight squeeze. But they finally acknowledged the booming business by doubling in size and now local slimmies find it easier to locate a lunchtime space at their favorite diet-food emporium. La Diet's appeal is food that's low in price as well as calories. There are always fresh fruit and vegetable salads, freshly made soups and even some sandwiches, as well as yogurt and calorie-counting shakes made with skim milk and ice milk flavored with fruit and honey.

LA DIET, 1634 Ludlow Street, Philadelphia. Telephone: (215) 564-2493. Hours: Monday-Friday 11 am-8 pm; Saturday 11 am-4 pm. No cards. No alcoholic beverages. Nearby parking garage.

The Athletic Club, Schuylkill Navy

57

## Philadelphia: East Philly
## LA FAMIGLIA
### Italian

**$$**

As the name proclaims, La Famiglia is a family-run restaurant featuring, from antipasti to dolci, the Sena family's specialties. Although the kitchen covers a lot of Italian territory, including Rome, Sicily, Florence and Venice, the emphasis seems to be on the food from Campania, that region just above the foot of Italy's boot. The carne pizzaiola, steak with oregano-flavored sauce, is the best-known beef dish in Naples. There is abundant use of anchovies, shellfish, peppers and mozzarella cheese—all Campanian favorites—throughout the menu. Capri comes into the picture with a veal recipe using cheese, spinach, pimiento and anchovy. Pompeii is represented with vitello Vesuvio, veal with prosciutto in marinara sauce. One of the delights of a meal here is the vitello Papa Sena, a sampler of three veal dishes from the menu, all of them delicious. The restaurant is attractively decorated, neat and friendly. Well-chosen Italian wines are available to complement the food.

LA FAMIGLIA, 8 South Front Street, Philadelphia. Telephone: (215) 922-2803. Lunch: Tuesday-Friday 11:30-2. Dinner: Tuesday-Saturday 5:30-10:30; Sunday 4:30-9. Closed Monday. Cards: AE, CB, MC, VISA. Reservations advised. Full bar service. Street parking.

## Vitello (veal)

*Vitello Combination Papa Sena* ~ Capri, Piccante, Mandolese... 10.95

*Vitello Mandolese* ~ Veal with Italian Cheese and Prosciutto, with Marsala Wine... 9.95

*Costata di Vitello* ~ Veal Chop Sauteed in Mushrooms and Green Peppers... 10.95

*Scaloppine Alla Siciliana* ~ Veal with Capers, Black Olives, in Wine Marinara Sauce... 8.50

*Vitello Vesuvio* ~ Veal with Prosciutto and Italian Cheese with Marinara White Wine... 8.95

*Saltimbocca · Alla Romana* ~ Rolled Veal with Cheese and Prosciutto in Marsala ... 8.95

*Vitello Capri* ~ Veal with Italian Cheese, Spinach, Pimentoes and Anchovies... 8.95

*Vitello Con Carciofi* ~ Veal with Artichoke in Butter, White Wine Sauce... 8.50

*Cotolette Alla Parmigiana* ~ Veal with Italian Cheese, Tomato Sauce... 8.25

*Cannellone* ~ Veal and Egg Wrapped in Crepe with Parmesan Cheese... 7.95

*Vitello Alla Panna* ~ Veal with Cream Butter Sauce, Black Pepper, and Parsley... 8.95

*Costolette Ai Ferri* ~ Veal Chop Broiled with Garlic... 10.95

## Carne (steak)

*Filetto Monte Carlo Papa Sena's* ~ Filet Steak with Block Pepper and Brandy... 11.95

*Filetto Alla Famiglia* ~ Filet Steak with Mushroom, Onion, Garlic and Wine Sauce... 11.95

*Carne Pizzaiola* ~ Sirloin Steak with Oregano and Pepper in Marinara Sauce... 11.95

## Pollo (Chicken)

*Involtini di Pollo* ~ Rolled Breast of Chicken with Italian Ham and Mozzarella, Wine and Mushrooms... 7.95

*Pollo Diavolo* ~ Half Chicken in Hot Sauce... 7.95

*Pollo Fiorentina* ~ Breast of Chicken on Bed of Spinach in Wine Sauce... 7.95

*Filetto di Pollo Romano* ~ Breast of Chicken with Cheese, Prosciutto in Marsala Wine... 7.95

*Petti di Pollo Piccante* ~ Breast of Chicken with Lemon and Butter Sauce... 7.25

## Pesce (seafood)

*Linguine Pescatore* ~ Linguine with Assorted Shellfish and White Sauce... 9.95

*Gamberi Famiglia* ~ Shrimp Fried in a Bed of Spinach in White Wine... 8.50

*Gamberi Romano* ~ Shrimp in White Wine and Lemon Sauce... 8.25

*Sogliola Cleopatra* ~ Broiled Filet of Flounder in Butter, Lemon, Shrimp Sauce... 8.95

*Aragosta Pompei* ~ Lobster Tail Dipped in Eggs with Butter, Wine Sauce... 11.95

*Merluzzo Al Forno* ~ Whiting with Vinegar Wine, Lemon and Garlic... 7.95

*Gamberoni Al Ferri* ~ Broiled Shrimp... 9.95

*Zuppa di Pesce* ~ Bouillabaisse, Italian Style (Wednesday & Friday)... 9.95

*Frittura di Pesce* ~ Pan Fried Calamari, Smelts, Shrimps... 8.95

# Philadelphia: North Philadelphia
## LA PAELLA
Spanish/Latin American  $$

That La Paella has survived and even thrived despite a location that is anything but fashionable says a lot about the food and the charm of this restaurant. What must have been a corner store in the Hispanic Logan neighborhood has been transformed into a cozy grotto with colorful cloths, dripping candles, touches of ceramic tile and tons of greenery, all convincing you you've wandered into flamenco land. La Paella got its start as a Portuguese restaurant, but when the original owner packed up his profits and headed back across the Atlantic, the kitchen acquired a new Spanish chef and some Spanish specialties like the sizzling seafood, poultry and meat dish for which the place is named. The paella here, to my mind at least, comes in second to the zarzuela, however. The latter, a somewhat similar fish and shellfish combination, has a far more intriguing brandied sauce. Also delicious at La Paella are the shrimp sautéed in garlic sauce, the fejoada (the national dish of Brazil) and the Portuguese pork and clams. La Paella's menu is large and nicely balanced between meat and seafood choices. Desserts include some wine-soaked fruits that taste canned or frozen even when they aren't and a rather good flan. For coffee, I suggest the espresso.

LA PAELLA, 1301 Rockland Street, Philadelphia. Telephone: (215) 455-7996. Hours: dinner from 4 pm. Closed Monday. No cards. Reservations advised. Wine only. Street parking.

## Spanish and Portuguese Cuisine

### Carnes - Meat Specialty

**Sirloin Steak Ala Pimienta Al Brandy** ............................ *11.50*
Specialty, pepper sirloin flambe Armagnac cream sauce.

**Medalion of Tenderloin Salteado Al Porto** ......................... *9.50*
Sliced filet sauted in Port wine, mushrooms, green peppers, onions.

**Entrecote Salteado Ala Tabernera Vinotinto** ....................... *9.75*
Prime sirloin steak in challots, mushrooms, peppers in red wine sauce.

**Loin Solomillo De Pork Marinado Ala Antejana** .................... *7.95*
Pork marinated with clams ala Antejana rose wine and brandy.

**Mixed Grill Mixto Especial De La Casa** ........................... *8.95*
House specialty, lamb, veal, liver, tenderloin, pork, saute in port wine sauce.

**Ternera Salteadas Tio Pepe** ..................................... *8.50*
Veal scallopini, challote mushrooms, cherri tio Pepe cream sauce.

**Calves Liver, Salteado Alisbonensa Salsa De Ajo** .................. *6.50*
Sliced, sauted garlic in red wine sauce

**Filet of Pork Ala Cardinal Salsa Portuguesa** ...................... *6.95*
Pork filet sauted in Cardinal sauce, garlic, peppers, onions, tomatoes, red wine
sauce.

**Costillitas De Cordero Le Chal Estoril** ........................... *7.75*
Baby Lamb chops sauted in green peppers, garlic in red wine sauce.

**Steak En Cubos A La Portuguesa Marsala** ......................... *8.75*
Cubes of beef in casserole and Portuguese style sauce.

### Pascados - Seafood Specialty

**Paella De Mariscos Ala Valenciana** ............................... *7.75*
Seafood combination tio Pepe - chicken, shrimp, scallops, King Crab, Clams,
Mussels, Spanish Rice, Chorizo and green peppers.

**Zarzuela, Costa Brava, Al Brandy** ............................... *8.50*
Superb dish from Barcelona, in Brandy Lobster sauce.

**Mariscada Mediterranea** ......................................... *8.50*
Seafood combination in Chabli wine sauce Portuguese style.

**Bacalao Ala Tio Pepe, Chef Specialty** ............................ *6.25*
Fresh Cod fish, red peppers, Chorizo, garlic, white chabli and tomato sauce.

**Langosta Viva Ala Antejana** .................................... :
Live Lobster, Port wine and Brandy sauce.

**Caserola Special Pepe, Camarones Y Vieras, Catalana** ............. *7.50*
Shrimp and Scallops, saute specialty, Pepe Brandy sauce.

**Camarones Salteados En Salsa De Langosta** ...................... *6.95*
Shrimp saute in Lobster and Brandy sauce

**Calamares Especiales Pepe Porto Y Brandy** ...................... *5.95*
Squid saute in Port Wine and Brandy Specialty Pepe.

SCALLOPS, SAUTE SPECIAL SAUCE ................ *6.75*

# LA PANETIÈRE
French $$$

With opera house-size crystal chandeliers, silk-shrouded walls and elegantly appointed tables, La Panetière is easily one of the country's most elegant meal settings. Look beyond the scenery and find the workmanlike output of a conscientious kitchen and the graceful service of a carefully rehearsed staff. La Panetière does best when it does the least, bringing superb quality ingredients to the table in much the same form as they arrived from the provisioner. Beluga caviar is presented with appropriate pomp, the full tin whisked from its nest in crushed ice, opened, admired, then silver-spooned to the plate in cabachon ovals. Salad is simple and perfect here, nothing but pale, unblemished leaves of tenderest lettuce with a classic dressing lightly filming each leaf. Order fresh raspberries and they'll be ripe, round and as dewy fresh as if they'd been picked that morning. La Panetière's flaws are subtle enough to be overlooked by a clientele that regularly includes local business and professional men and lawyers with out-of-town contacts to impress, divorcées testing a prospect's wallet and interest and college students being indulged by wealthy parents. The wine list slips in a few affordable bottles for their "I've been saving all year for this" customers.

LA PANETIÈRE, 1602 Locust Street, Philadelphia. Telephone: (215) 546-5452. Lunch: Monday-Friday 12-2. Dinner: Monday-Saturday 6-9:30. Closed Sunday. Cards: AE, DC. Full bar service. Reservations advised. Parking lot nearby.

## LES POTAGES

| | |
|---|---|
| POTAGE DU JOUR | 4.00 |
| VICHYSSOISE | 4.50 |
| SOUPE DE ST. JACQUES AU SAFRAN | 6.00 |
| BISQUE DE HOMARD | 7.00 |

## LES HORS D'OEUVRE

| | |
|---|---|
| POMME DE TERRE EN SURPRISE | 12.00 |
| SAUMON FUMÉ D'ÉCOSSE | 11.00 |
| CAVIAR BELUGA | 35.00 |
| TERRINE DE CANARD | 6.00 |
| TOAST A LA MOELLE | 6.00 |
| MOUSSE DE CREVETTES AUX JULIENNES | 7.50 |
| QUICHE A LA TOMATE, NIÇOISE | 5.50 |
| BOUCHÉE AUX RIS DE VEAU | 8.00 |
| MOULES AUX ÉPINARDS (POUR DEUX) | 11.00 |
| SALADE DE BIBB | 3.50 |
| SALADE ENDIVE OU MIMOSA | 5.00 |

## LES POISSONS

| | |
|---|---|
| ESPADON GRILLÉ, SAUCE BERNAISE | 14.00 |
| GOUJONETTES DE SOLE | 13.50 |
| COQUILLES ST. JACQUES AU BEURRE BLANC | 15.00 |
| SOLE DE LA MANCHE, A VOTRE FACON | 16.00 |
| HOMARD GRILLÉ, OU THERMIDOR | 24.00 |

## LES ENTREES

| | |
|---|---|
| MIGNON DE VEAU ORLOFF, EN CROÛTE | 16.00 |
| POULET AU VINAIGRE A L'ESTRAGON | 14.00 |
| CHOIX DE GIBIER EN PERIODE DE CHASSE | 16.00 |
| DELICE DE POULARD AUX MORILLES | 15.00 |
| AIGUILLETTES DE CANARD | 15.50 |
| CAILLES AU NID | 16.00 |
| TRANCHES DE JAMBON MORVANDELLE | 12.00 |
| NOISETTES D'AGNEAU ARLÉSIENNE | 16.00 |
| CARRÉ D'AGNEAU (POUR DEUX) | 36.00 |
| FOIE DE VEAU BERCY | 14.00 |
| ENTRE CÔTE A LA MOELLE (POUR DEUX) | 38.00 |
| CÔTE DE VEAU PROVENÇALE | 38.00 |
| TOURNEDOS POÊLE AUX TROIS MOUTARDES | 16.00 |
| FILET AUX POIVRES | 16.00 |
| RIS DE VEAU FLORENTINE | 14.00 |
| FAISAN, SAUCE SMITANE (POUR DEUX) | 30.00 |

## Philadelphia: East Philly
## THE LATEST DISH
Cosmopolitan                                              $$

The owners of the Latest Dish describe the output of their
kitchen as "American cosmopolitan," and they work to
keep the dishes simple yet satisfying. The restaurant was
once an old-fashioned bakery and, except for touches of
neon and greenery, it still looks the part. Stamped-tin
ceilings provide an overhead view. Walls are shiny white tile.
There's a deep, old-fashioned display window giving front
tables a view of the street scene (and strollers a view of the
front tables.) One of the menu listings that changes fre-
quently is the Ultra Dish. On the day of a recent visit, the
"latest" was a marvelous stir-fried beef dish that consisted
of a large portion of finger-sized strips of tender beef with
lots of wonderful, crisp-cooked vegetables and rice in an
interesting tamari-based sauce. Rack of lamb, a second
entrée sampled, was a rather large rack of thyme-scented rib
chops that arrived slightly overcooked. Desserts were fresh
baked banana cake buried beneath a snow slide of whipped
cream and an excellent, though homely, German chocolate
cake. In addition to the main dining area, the Latest Dish
has a second-floor room that becomes a disco starting at 10
every evening.

THE LATEST DISH, 613 South Fourth Street, Philadel-
phia. Telephone: (215) 925-1680. Hours: daily from 6
pm-2 am; Sunday brunch 1-10 pm. Cards: AE, MC, VISA.
Reservations advised. Full bar service. Street parking.

**Philadelphia: East Philly**
**LA TRUFFE**
French

# $$$

If you're looking for a romantic restaurant, one that's as pretty and flower-filled as a French country house in spring, you couldn't do better than this riverfront-area gem. But beyond the valentine trappings beats the heart of a serious kitchen, which is why the restaurant does consistently well with local and visiting business people. Francophiles will enjoy eavesdropping on conversations between French-speaking waiters who also explain the menu for those who find the lack of English translations disconcerting. The offerings are classic, often classy. Dinner hors d'oeuvre include beluga caviar and truffled salad. Beyond that, the range of selections is fairly standard for an upper-price-range French restaurant. There's duck done with olives, veal kidney with mustard saucing, veal with morel mushrooms. Lunch is equally predictable with a little something for everyone from omelets to lamb chops.

LA TRUFFE, 10 South Front Street, Philadelphia. Telephone: (215) 627-8630. Lunch: Tuesday-Friday 12-2. Dinner: Monday-Saturday 6-11; closed Sunday. Cards: AE, DC, MC, VISA. Reservations advised. Full bar service. Street parking.

| | |
|---|---:|
| Faisan Saint-Hubert | 2800 |
| Canard braisé au poivre vert | 1350 |
| Coquelet Mirabelle | 1250 |
| Côtelette de veau Périgueux | 1550 |
| Rognons de veau Bérichon | 1000 |
| Carré d'agneau au jus (pour deux) | 3250 |
| Tournedos à l'estragon | 1600 |
| Entrecôte aux chanterelles | 1550 |

# Philadelphia: West Philadelphia
## LA TERRASSE
French                                          $$

In 1966, La Terrasse set up shop at the end of a row of Victorian townhouses in a neighborhood near the University of Pennsylvania. It was a remarkable restaurant then and remains so for several reasons. One is the staff, a lively mix of attractive, articulate young people, many of whom work here to support artistic or scholastic endeavors. The customer mix is another fascination. It includes scientists and engineers, professors and poets, medical miracle-workers (from several nearby hospitals), as well as neighborhood joggers. There's more. A Steinway grand fills the place with music regularly. A glass-enclosed terrace, heated as well as is possible in winter, lets you check in with nature whatever the weather. If there's an occasional chill, blame the twin roof holes that permit a pair of tall trees to spread their branches over the whole whimsical operation. La Terrasse was one of the first local restaurants to offer Sunday brunch and many feel it's still the best place to come. Seasonings for your eggs Florentine routinely include live Mozart played by a young, terribly earnest chamber group. Food quality has been uneven over the years, but the current chef is a talented young Thai who shows signs of keeping the kitchen output stable. The menu is a fairly conventional French list with lots of nice touches. (Escargots arrive in garlic butter on spinach topped with Gruyère.) If you're looking for a late snack, La Terrasse obliges with a modestly priced menu and an excellent bar.

LA TERRASSE, 3432 Sansom Street, Philadelphia. Telephone: (215) 387-3778. Lunch: Monday-Friday 11:30-2:30. Dinner: Monday-Saturday 6-11; Sunday to 10. Friday and Saturday late supper 11-1. Sunday brunch noon-3. Cards: AE, DC, MC, VISA. Reservations advised. Full bar service. Street parking and nearby lots at 34th and Chestnut, 36th and Walnut.

## Bar Provençal en Papillote  9.95
*Fresh sea bass cooked in parchment paper with
tomatoes, garlic, capers, black olives, and spices*

## Canard Rôti  9.00
*Half a roast duck with a seasonal sauce*

## Poulet au Cari  8.25
*Chicken sauteed with sweet peppers and potatoes
in a curried cream sauce*

## Côtelettes de Poularde La Terrasse  8.95
*Boneless breasts of chicken sauteed in butter
and baked with proscuitto ham and gruyere cheese,
served in madeira wine sauce with morels*

## Escalopes de Porc au Vin Blanc  9.25
*Escalopes of pork sauteed in white wine
with shallots and mushrooms*

## Veau à la Normande  9.50
*Escalopes of veal sauteed in butter, flambeed
in apple brandy, and served in a cream sauce
with sliced apples*

## Filet de Boeuf Poivre Verte  12.50
*Filet mignon wrapped in bacon served in a
red wine sauce with whole green peppercorns*

## Philadelphia: East Philly
## LAUTREC AND CAFÉ BORGIA
### French/Italian

**$$$**

This is a small but caring restaurant, one that pays exquisite attention to detail. At a recent lunch the stemmed glasses in which our dry sherry arrived were expensively thin and polished to a sparkling fare-thee-well. There were crisp-fresh miniature carnations on the table and interesting lithographs on the walls. The background music was classical and quiet. The food is prepared with equal concern for all the senses. Lautrec's Sunday brunch, one of the city's most popular, starts with a glass of freshly squeezed orange or grapefruit juice. It features a choice of omelets, made at tableside. There's wine, some excellent fresh bread and rolls with sweet butter. For a fitting finish in the French manner, you're brought oranges, chocolate and mocha java. The dinner card is small but has several unusual choices. There's pheasant in a tart orange sauce and pork chops with white peaches. The Lautrec menu asks diners to refrain from smoking cigars or pipes. It also states that a 15-percent gratuity will be added to the check. If that seems too restrictive or too pricey for your pocketbook, owner Ed Bottone will direct you to his more affordable, casual Café Borgia next door. At the Borgia, the menu features soups, light dishes like quiche and pâté, cheese assortments, omelets, burgers, crêpes and sandwiches, plus some rather elegant desserts. A small selection of modestly priced wines is available at the café. A larger, more comprehensive wine list can be found at Lautrec.

LAUTREC, 408 South Second Street, Philadelphia. Telephone: (215) 923-6660. Dinner: Tuesday-Saturday 6-10. Sunday brunch 11-2:30. (Café Borgia hours: Tuesday-Saturday 6 pm-1 am; Sunday 4 pm-10 pm. Sunday brunch 11:30-3.) Cards: AE. Reservations advised. Full bar service. Street parking.

## Cannelloni    8⁷⁵
tubes of pasta stuffed with veal and cheese.
Sauce mornay.

## Tortellini con crema e piselli    6⁹⁵
meat filled pockets of pasta in a cream
sauce of locatelli cheese and peas.

## Poissons
our selection of fishes varies with freshness
and availability.

## Poulet au Curry    10⁹⁵
breast of Perdue chicken in a curry cream sauce
with raisins, fresh fruit and toasted almonds.

## Faisan Bigarade au Grand Marnier
succulent pheasant in a tart orange sauce    for two 24⁰⁰

## Petti di Anitra con Marsala    12⁷⁵
breast of duck with prosciutto in a
marvelous Marsala wine sauce.

## Cotelettes de Porc
aux peches blanches
tender center cut pork chops with white peaches.    11⁷⁵

## Carré d'Agneau au Poivre Vert    14⁹⁵
roast rack of baby lamb prepared with
Dijon mustard & rosemary. A brown sauce
with Madagascar green pepper corns.

## Medallions de Veau    14²⁵
aux Chanterelles
veal medallions in cream with swiss mushrooms.

## Bistecca Cesare Borgia    12⁷⁵
alternating slices of filet of beef and layers
of spinach bechamel. Something special.

## Noisettes d'Agneau Bernard    15²⁵
sliced filet of lamb in a mustard cream
sauce laced with Armagnac.

## Philadelphia: Center City
## LE BEC FIN
French

$$$

In years of hearing Le Bec Fin lavishly praised, I can remember only one complaint and that from a woman reader who had heard it was the most expensive restaurant in town and, based on that, had booked a table for a wedding anniversary. "It was awful," she wrote. "All that money and they didn't have any music." No, Le Bec Fin's owner-chef Georges Perrier can't hum the Anniversary Waltz, but the dynamic Frenchman does cook so well that even competitive chefs concede he is the local king of haute cuisine. Perrier has the right combination of talent and training but he also works long and hard. He scorns short-cuts, prowls the markets coaxing choicest provisions from the butcher, the baker, the fruit man, the vegetable vender. And, because he buys the best, a prix fixe of $44 a person is the only way he can stay in business, he claims. Sauces, like the wine and cream delight splashed over caviar-topped sole, are invariably simple-seeming, yet as rich and appropriate as real pearls worn with a Norell suit. Le Bec Fin oysters are cooked just until the tender edges curl like layered chiffon, then they're perfumed with a mysterious herbal bouquet. Snails romp with hazelnuts in tiny copper tubs

Coquille St Jacques au Poivre Vert

Barbue Braisé Sauce Champagne

Mousse aux Deux Sauces

Espadon Provençale en Papillote

Escargots au Champagne

Cervelas de Fruits de Mer

Quenelle de Brochet
Sauce Homard

bubbling with butter. But the real glory of the kitchen is the quenelles, simple, squat shapes of fish, pulverized, sieved, then folded into beaten eggs and butter with so light a touch that the whole fragile creation threatens to collapse under the whisper weight of the sauce. The menu changes with the seasons but there's usually something to please even the person who is not a fan of "fancy foods." Rack of lamb, for example. A small wedge from each of several perfectly ripened cheeses. Or a serving of frozen Grand Marnier soufflé that tastes like ice cream gone to heaven. Service matches the food. Your selection is wheeled to your table on an appropriately decorated cart and shown to you before the waiter arranges it on your fine china plate. Wine service is handled with equal finesse. The list is fairly extensive and if you find it confusing, ask for a translation or suggestion. Since the restaurant is small and there is no reception area, try not to arrive before the time of your reservation or you may find yourself waiting in the heat or cold of the street until your table is ready.

LE BEC FIN, 1312 Spruce Street, Philadelphia. Telephone: (215) 732-3000. Hours: Monday-Saturday 6 pm-9 pm. No cards. Reservations advised. Full bar service. Parking lot next door.

*Pigeon Le Bec-Fin*
*Poulet Cynthia*
*Le Gibier de Pays*
*Piece d'Agneau en Croûte*
*Entrecôte pour deux*
*Sauce Périgourdine*
*Ris de Veau Sauce Financière*
*Medaillon de Veau Sauce Nantaise*
*Filet de Boeuf Valancia*

## Philadelphia: East Philly
## LE BISTRO
French                                              $$

Le Bistro's latest crowd-pleaser is Rick's Caberet, a name given to the new, plant-filled, glass-walled room recently added to expand the tiny bar/restaurant's breathing space. At Rick's, or anywhere at Le Bistro for that matter, the dining is only mildly adventurous. The small selection of appetizers runs to soups and such staples as quiche and pâté. The six entrées include steak with spicy tomato sauce, trout stuffed with almonds, sour cream and fennel, duck with an orange glaze. Desserts include a variety of home-made cakes and pastries. Late snackers have their own menu, again, fairly conventional. It includes omelets, hamburgers served on French bread, a cheese platter and quiche, as well as soups, salads and desserts.

LE BISTRO, 757 South Front Street, Philadelphia. Telephone: (215) 389-3855. Dinner: Tuesday-Sunday 5-11; late supper to 1 am. Sunday brunch 1 pm-4 pm. Cards: AE, House, MC, VISA. Reservations advised. Full bar service. Street parking. Jazz entertainment nightly.

## Potages

| | |
|---|---|
| SOUP DU JOUR | 1²⁵ |
| SOUP A L'OIGNON | 1⁵⁰ |
| Onion Soup, Gratinee | |
| SOUP DE POISSON | 1⁵⁰ |
| Fish Soup | |

## Hors D'Oeuvre

| | |
|---|---|
| PATE DU CHEF | 2⁵⁰ |
| ESCARGOT | 3⁹⁵ |
| Snails in Garlic Butter | |
| LEGUMES VINAIGRETTE | 2⁷⁵ |
| Cold Marinated Vegetables | |
| QUICHE DU JOUR | 2⁵⁰ |

## Salades

| | |
|---|---|
| SALADE BISTRO | 1⁷⁵ |
| Vinaigrette Salad | |
| SALADE CESAR | 2⁵⁰ |
| Caesar Salad | |

| | |
|---|---|
| CHAMPIGNONS A LA CESAR | 2⁵⁰ |
| Fresh Mushrooms on lettuce with Caesar dressing | |
| SALADE VINAIGRETTE | 1⁰⁰ |
| Tossed Greens and tomato | |

## Entrees

**BIFTECK** SAUCE PROVENÇAL
Sauted Strip Steak,  8 oz 10⁵⁰
with Spicy Tomato Sauce  12 oz 12⁵⁰

**CANARD** A L'ORANGE 8⁹⁵
Roast Long Island Duckling
with Orange Sauce

**FILET MIGNON** SAUCE PERIGUEUX
12⁵⁰
Filet of Tenderloin,
Sauted with Madeira and Truffle Sauce

**POULET** SAUTE AUX FINES HERBES
7²⁵
Boneless Breast of Chicken
sauted with white wine, shallots and herbs, served
with an artichoke bottom.

**ESCALOPES** DE **VEAU** ALMONDINE
8⁵⁰
Veal Scallops,
sauted with lemon, rind parsley, breadcrumbs
and almonds

**TRUITE** FARCIE 6²⁵
Sauteed Boneless Trout
stuffed with sour cream, almonds, fennel,

## Philadelphia: East Philly
## LE CHAMPIGNON
### French

**$$**

Le Champignon is a homey French restaurant with rough ceiling beams, walls covered with farm implements and lots of country charm. It is also a stylish, formal restaurant with white cloths, silk lampshades and a certain dignity. In addition to the restaurant's two, distinctly different dining rooms, Le Champignon aims to please with a choice of robust country cooking, classic French and even imaginative nouvelle cuisine dishes. In the last category are stuffed chicken breast served with light curry sauce, roast duck under a sweet and sour plum sauce, scallops spiked with fennel. On the classics list find quenelles de brochet (ultra-light pike dumplings under a shellfish sauce), poached salmon with cucumber, rack of lamb scented with rosemary and thyme. The restaurant takes pride in its inexpensive French house wines.

LE CHAMPIGNON, 122 Lombard Street, Philadelphia. Telephone: (215) 925-1106. Lunch: Monday-Friday 12-2:30. Dinner: 5:30-11; Saturday to midnight; Sunday 4-9. Cards: AE, VISA. Reservations advised. Full bar service. Street parking.

## Les Poissons

FILET DE SOLE FARÇIS AU CRABE.................10.00
    *stuffed sole with crab meat, mushroom, lobster sauce*

TRUITE FERMIERE AUX CHAMPIGNONS............ 9.00
    *stuffed trout*

DARNE DE SAUMON POCHÉ......................... 9.00
    *poached salmon, cucumber sauce*

COQUILLE ST. JACQUES BERCY..................... 9.00
    *scallops, white wine, cream sauce, fenell*

MOULES FLORENTINE............................. 9.00
    *mussels, mushrooms, white wine sauce, bed of spinach*

HOMARD SYLVANIE (priced according to season) ....
    *lobster—house specialty*

BOUILLABAISSE DE MARSEILLE....................11.00
    *combination, fresh fish, shell fish, lobster, safron soup*

CREVETTES SAUTE PARISIENNE.................... 11.50
    *large sauted shrimps in garlic, tomato, onion, lemon*

GRENOUILLES PROVENÇALES..................... 10.50
    *frog legs, garlic sauce*

## Les Volailles

COQUELET AUX GROSEILLES...................... 8.50
    *cornish hen, currants, white wine sauce*

POULET FARÇIS A L'INDIENNE..................... 8.00
    *stuffed chicken breast, light curry sauce*

COQ AU VIN...................................... 8.00
    *marinated chicken in red wine sauce*

CANARD AUX PRUNES............................ 9.00
    *duck, sweet and sour plum sauce*

CANARD MONTMORENCY......................... 9.00
    *duck, black cherry sauce*

## Les Viandes

ENTRECOTE BORDELAISE......................... 13.00
    *sirlon, echalotte, wine sauce*

STEAK AU POIVRE............................... 13.00
    *sirlon, mustard, pepper sauce, cognac*

TOURNEDOS HENRY IV........................... 13.50
    *filet mignon, bearnaise sauce*

ESCALLOPE DE VEAU A L'ALSASSIENNE............ 12.00
    *sliced veal, white wine, capers, mushroom*

CARRÉ D'AGNEAU PERSILLÉ (for two)............... 26.00
    *rack of lamb roasted, rosemary, thyme, port wine sauce*

## Philadelphia: Center City
## LES AMIS
## Continental

**$$$**

Les Amis' decor is classic Bauhaus modern softened by the fresh flowers on the tables and the equally fresh art (often by the restaurant's waiters) on the walls. Vicky Rensen is the Danish owner. Chef Michael Scott is the young American trained in classic French cuisine who commands the kitchen. The result of this mini United Nations is a meal that might start with Scandinavian fruit soup (apricot is a favorite) or smoked trout with horseradish sauce, then turn French with truite meunière or nouvelle French with roast duck with curry and honey. The restaurant is particularly popular with men for lunch. The midday fare includes several substantial *plats,* including sautéed calves liver lyonnaise, pork chop with prune and apples (Danish style) and pôt au feu. Appropriate wines are available.

LES AMIS, 1920 Chestnut Street, Philadelphia. Telephone: (215) 567-0855. Lunch: Monday-Friday 12-2. Dinner: Monday-Friday 6-9:30; Saturday 6-10; Sunday 5-8. Cards: AE, DC, MC, VISA. Reservations advised. Full bar service. Nearby parking lots.

## HORS d'ŒUVRE

Ragoût de Morilles en chausson (Creamed morels in puff pastry) — 5.75

Croustade de Crevettes à la Rothschild (Shrimp in crouton) — 4.75

Quiche à l'oignon Alsacienne (Alsatian onion quiche) — 3.50

Pâté à ma Façon (Chef's pâté) — 3.50

Céleries aux Remoulade (Celery root with herbed mayonnaise sauce) — 3.00

Toasts à la Moëlle (Poached marrow on toast) — 3.75

Salade d'Endive (Belgian endive salad) — 3.00

## LES POTAGES

Soupe d'Abricot froid (Cold apricot soup) — 3.00

Potage Saint-Germain (Green pea soup) — 3.00

Consommé de Volaille au Basilic (Chicken consommé with basil) — 3.00

## LES POISSONS

Truite fumée Raifort (Smoked trout with horseradish sauce) — 4.50

Mousseline de Brochet (Mousse of pike) — 3.75

Coquilles Saint-Jacques au beurre blanc (Scallops in butter sauce) — 4.25

## LES PLATS

Pigeon Albufara (Squab stuffed with rice and foie gras) — 16.75

Truite Meunière (Sautéed trout with lemon butter) — 10.50

Gratin de Crabe aux Épinards (Creamed lump crabmeat over spinach) — 11.50

Grillades de Porc à la Dijonnaise (Slices of pork with mustard sauce) — 9.50

Côte de Veau Zingara (Veal chops with ham, mushrooms, and Madeira sauce) — 13.00

Rognons de Veau aux Flageoles (Kidneys with lima beans) — 8.75

Carré d'Agneau Persillé (Rack of lamb with mustard, breadcrumbs and parsley) — 15.00

Poulet Sauté au Riesling pour deux (Sautéed chicken immersed in wine w/cream for two) — 19.00

Canard à l'Indienne pour deux (Roast duck with honey and curry for two) — 22.00

Caille en Pâté Antonin Carême (Quail w/liver mousse in pastry, sauce Périgueux) — 18.50

## LES DESSERTS — 3.00

Café – .75          Thé – .60          Espresso – 1.00

## LICKETY SPLIT
International                                    $$

At Lickety Split, the entertainment starts the minute you're seated. The plate-glass window that makes up one long wall of this former retail store, lets you look out on a fascinating parade of tourists, local artists and neighborhood types, including city-wise dogs and cats. (The looking works both ways, incidentally, so don't be surprised to see a drooling Great Dane eyeballing your filet mignon.) The restaurant's menu offers an assortment of good soups (my favorite is the Bulgarian cucumber with walnuts and dill), an interesting salad, which the menu describes as "divine" (it includes raisins and sunflower seeds as well as fresh vegetables) and a selection of excellent desserts. The latter are baked exclusively for Lickety Split by an enterprising and talented young woman. Her recent output ranged from chocolate mousse in chocolate cups to walnut roulade and and Key lime pie. In addition to desserts, Lickety Split puts out a dandy sweet-tooth satisfier in the form of their fresh strawberry and banana daiquiris. The restaurant's late closing makes it a popular after-theater destination.

LICKETY SPLIT, South Street at Fourth, Philadelphia. Telephone: (215) 922-1173. Hours: Monday-Thursday 6 pm-midnight; Friday and Saturday to 1 am; Sunday dinner from 5 pm. Cards: AE, DC, MC, VISA. Reservations accepted. Full bar service. Street parking.

# Entrees

## chicken cubano
marinated in lime, sauteed in garlic & butter   6.95

## chicken teriyaki
an old lickety favorite, skewered w/veggies & grilled 6.95

## stuffed flounder
baked in parchment, filled w/backfin crabmeat   7.50

## duck l'orange
½ roasted L.I. duckling w/an orange-curry glaze 8.75

## seafood crepe royale
crabmeat & scallops in a crepe w/a cheese sauce 8.95

## filet mignon
w/bearnaise or "au poivre" (powdered w/peppercorns) 9.50

## veal spiedini
thinly sliced veal, wrapped around prosciutto &
    and mozzarello, breaded, skewered & broiled.  11.50

## rack of lamb   for one
four baby lamb chops, baked w/lickety's own
    dijon-garlic dressing.    priced accordingly.

## LOS AMIGOS
Mexican                                              $

Los Amigos means "the friends" and it's an appropriate name for this small, cheerful Mexican restaurant. Los Amigos has rough-plastered white walls, brown vinyl leatherlike tablecloths, terra-cotta tile floors, a long attractive bar and a following that includes lots of attractive, friendly young people. It's a place where you go to relax and unwind, to eat heartily rather than exquisitely. Portions are plentiful. Food arrives on individual pottery well-and-tree platters rather than dinner plates. Not everything here will make you jump for joy; the guacamole is fresh and you get a whopping portion, but the flavor is flat, unaugmented by onion, garlic or spices in any detectable amount. Recommended are the tacos, the cheese enchilada, the refried beans and the burrito. Two dandy desserts are the delicate mango cream—soothing after a fiery Mexican meal —and a tantalizingly smooth flan. The bar mixes everything from margaritas to martinis, but with this food try an imported beer. Brazilian Brahma Chopp is my favorite.

LOS AMIGOS, 50 South Second Street, Philadelphia. Telephone: (215) 922-7061. Hours: Monday-Thursday 11:30 am-midnight; Friday and Saturday to 1 am. Closed Sunday. All major cards. Full service bar open to 2 am. Street parking.

**AZTEC**—chicken taco, beef taco, cheese enchilada, guacamole salad, rice and beans .......................................... **5.25**

**EL BANDITO**—tamale, chicken taco, cheese enchilada refried beans and rice .......................................... **4.75**

**OMELETTE MEXICANO**—stuffed with onions, peppers, olives, mild chiles and cheese, served with rice and beans .................. **3.95**

**CARNE TAMPIQUENA**—steak mexican style with corn tortillas, rice and beans, guacamole salad .............................. **6.25**

**TACO PLATE**—choice of any three, chicken, beef, avacado, or bean served with rice and beans ................................... **3.95**

**ENCHILADA PLATE**—choice of any three, chicken, beef, avacado, or cheese served with rice and beans ........................... **3.95**

**TOLTEC**—beef taco, chicken enchilada served with rice and beans, guacamole salad ............................................ **4.25**

**BURRITO PLATE**—two burritos, served with rice .................... **3.75**

**CHILE RELLENO PLATE**—topped with sour cream, served with rice and beans .................................................. **5.25**

**ENCHILADA VERDES**—chicken enchiladas topped with green sauce and sour cream, served with rice and beans .................. **4.25**

**TAMALE PLATE**—two tamales served with rice and beans ........... **4.25**

**QUESADILLA GRANDE**—flour tortilla stuffed with beef, green pepper, onion, cheese, lettuce, tomato and sour cream served with rice and beans ................................... **3.75**

**HUACHINANGO a la VERACRUZANA**—red snapper prepared Veracruz style, served with rice and beans .................... **5.75**

**ARROZ CON POLLO**—chicken in a spicy red sauce served on Mexican rice with beans and guacamole salad .......................... **3.95**

**TOSTADA PLATE**—chicken and beef tostada served with rice ......... **3.95**

# Philadelphia: East Philly
## LUIGI'S TRATTORIA
### Italian

**$$**

Twelve years ago, when the doors to this traditional trattoria opened, Luigi's had the neighborhood to itself. It was before the development of New Market, before the Society Hill real estate superboom, before the city's restaurant renaissance. Now, of course, the city in general and this area specifically teems with restaurants of every ethnic persuasion. Neither the proliferation of choices nor the competition with those offering the newly fashionable northern Italian cuisine has kept Luigi's from prospering. What the kitchen does best is wonderfully substantial mamma mia stuff like homemade pasta, lasagne, gnocchi, mussels, oysters and clams in rich garlicky sauces, roast peppers and Italian cream cakes. There are daily changes in the menu. Squid, stuffed or simmered in spicy tomato sauce, is often included. The list of special chicken and veal dishes is certain to contain some of your favorites. Fresh fish combinations also abound. There's even honeycomb tripe in tomato sauce for the adventurous.

LUIGI'S TRATTORIA, 511 South Second Street, Philadelphia. Telephone: (215) 923-6898. Lunch: Monday-Friday 11:30-2:30. Dinner: Monday-Friday 5-9; Saturday 5-10; Sunday 2:30-8:30. Cards: AE, DC, MC, VISA. Reservations advised. Full bar service. Parking lot.

| | |
|---|---:|
| Boneless Breast of Chicken Valdostano, Served with Greens | 7.00 |
| Veal Bundlette, Served with Fettucchini Verde | 8.00 |
| Bracciole of Beef Napoletano, Served with Gnocchi | 7.00 |
| Sweetbreads Saute in Sherry Wine Sauce with Mushrooms | 6.75 |
| Veal Cutlet Parmigiana, Served with Spaghetti | 7.50 |
| Chicken Cacciatore | 6.50 |
| Sausage Cacciatore | 6.00 |
| Scaloppini Di Vitello Piccante, Served with Greens and Potato Croquette | 8.00 |
| Scaloppini Di Vitello with Mushrooms and Peppers | 7.50 |
| Scaloppini Di Vitello in Marsala Wine With Mushrooms and Potato Croquette | 8.00 |
| Baked Shrimp Trattoria | 7.00 |
| Filet of Flounder Fiorentina, Served with Greens | 7.50 |
| Blue Fish Mediterranean | 7.00 |
| Calamoli Ripieni, Stuffed Squid | 6.75 |
| Calamoli Pomodoro, Squid in Tomato Sauce | 6.50 |
| Trippa Pomodora, Honey Comb Tripe in Tomato Sauce | 5.50 |
| Broiled Chicken (1/2), Served with A Vegetable | 7.00 |
| Broiled Pork Chops, Served with A Vegetable | 8.75 |
| Broiled Sirloin Steak, Served with A Vegetable | 10.00 |
| Filet Mignon, Served with A Vegetable | 10.50 |
| Steak Pizzaiola, Served with A Vegetable | 10.50 |

## Philadelphia: East Philly
## MAXWELL'S PRIME
## Steaks $$

White plates, white linens, white menus and wine lists with unvarnished descriptions set the scene for this new Philadelphia steak house. Nothing—but nothing—is allowed to steal the spotlight from the food here, which features—in addition to prime, aged beef—fresh fish and fresh vegetables. Service by crisply attired waiters is more professional than one might expect from an area (South Street) where it would not be unusual for your jeans-clad waiter or waitress to pull up a chair and join your dinner conversation.

MAXWELL'S PRIME, 623-625 South Street, Philadelphia. Telephone: (215) 923-6363. Hours: dinner nightly from 5:30 pm. Closed Monday. All major cards. Reservations advised. Full bar service. Street parking.

## Philadelphia: East Philly
## MARRAKESH
Moroccan

**$$**

Like my favorite restaurant in the city of Marrakesh, this one is on a narrow street that is not exactly easy to find. (Native Philadelphians have been known to consult a city map but you won't need to if you know in advance that Leithgow runs between Fourth and Fifth Streets and that the address on Leithgow is between Lombard and South.) One knocks at a massive wooden door to gain entrance to a small dining room wrapped in Moroccan rugs. Tables are low, hammered-brass circles that revolve to facilitate service. Seating is on low, pillowed and quite comfortable U-shaped benches around those tables. You eat Moroccan style here, with the fingers on your right hand. But first hands are washed with warm water poured from a brass kettle. Three salads make up the meal's introduction. They may include carrot circles, an eggplant-based mixture and cucumber. With them you eat bread that comes to the table in a massive, dome-lidded basket. Bastilla, an egg-and-poultry-filled pastry, which is a national dish in Morocco, arrives next. It is dusted with confectioners' sugar, traced with cinnamon in a lattice design. It is also finger-licking hot. But that is the Moroccan way and pulling the phyllo-pastry-wrapped pie apart becomes part of the lively enjoyment of the meal. Lemon chicken is the next course. It is made with salt-cured, tame lemons and big green olives. From here the meal goes to skewered, nicely seasoned lamb cubes. Couscous is the finale. It will disappoint only in that it doesn't mound up in the hand for eating as it would if it were made with the Moroccan grain. It is otherwise dandy, flavored with zucchini, turnips, carrots, raisins and peppery hot sauce. After fresh fruit and nuts (a basket is brought to your table), there's sticky, syrupy pastry and hot mint tea. The tea is super sweet and poured by your waiter from a kettle poised about a yard above your glass. Not to worry. His aim appears flawless.

MARRAKESH, 517 South Leithgow, Philadelphia. Telephone: (215) 925-5929. Hours: nightly 6 pm-11 pm. No cards. Reservations essential. Bring your own wine. Street parking.


## Philadelphia: East Philly
## THE MARKET FAIR
International $

The Market Fair is Philadelphia's 20th century equivalent of the food stalls of a Middle Eastern bazaar. Located in the Gallery, a modern, enclosed downtown shopping area, the Market Fair boasts more than 20 different food stands that offer an international feast all can afford. As an experiment, with $10 in my pocket, I set out to discover how much food I could collect for sampling from the Fair's subterranean maze. I also wanted to know if the food would be worth even the modest amount I was willing to spend. The answer to the first question was: German franks with kraut and mustard; New England clam chowder; all-American charcoal-broiled hamburger; Mexican tacos, burritos and enchiladas; Sicilian pizza; Greek rice-stuffed grape leaves and nut-filled baklava and Chinese chicken wings. To the second, I can only say that my taste panel gobbled up the whole collection with gusto. The food stands also feature a raw seafood bar, health-food counter and crêpe corner. Pick up your selections and carry them to the center of the area where there are seats for snackers. Occasionally street musicians will provide a mealtime serenade.

THE MARKET FAIR IN THE GALLERY, Market Street from Ninth to 11th, Philadelphia. Hours: Monday-Saturday 9 am-9 pm; Sunday 11:30 am-5 pm. No cards. Cocktails and wine available. Adjoining garage.

## Philadelphia: East Philly
## MIDDLE EAST RESTAURANT
Middle Eastern                                              $

Lamb—baked, broiled, fried and even raw—is the food focus of the lively family-owned Middle East Restaurant. The fun focuses on belly dancers, native music and waiters in red fez and vest. The menu wanders all over the Middle East, with stopovers in Lebanon, Syria, Jordan, Iraq, Egypt, the Arabian Peninsula and Israel. For under $10 there are budget feasts that include homus or eggplant caviar, Lebanese salad, stuffed grape and cabbage leaves, rice pilaff, coffee (a choice of Turkish or infidel) and an entrée like shish kabob. Greek pastitos (macaroni, ground meat and egg custard) or something *really* exotic like stuffed eggplant slices. Late-night snackers can also order kibbee, the excellent ground lamb dish from Lebanon, or vegetarian appetizer platters. The whole Tayoun family pitches in at the restaurant. Mom cooks almost everything, but the pastries are Pop's specialty. His contributions include diamond-shaped baklava said to contain 60 layers of pastry as well as syrup and nuts, and crescent maa-a-mul, made of semolina with nuts or fruits. Both are very sweet and best accompanied with a thimble of the Middle East's thick, strong Turkish coffee. The restaurant offers a 20-plate smorgasbord that feeds four at a fixed price of under $20. There's an infidel menu as well.

MIDDLE EAST RESTAURANT, 126 Chestnut Street, Philadelphia. Telephone: (215) 922-1003. Lunch: Monday-Saturday 11 am-3 pm. Dinner: Sunday-Saturday 5 pm-2 am. Cards: AE, CB, DC, MC, VISA. Reservations accepted. Full bar service. Street parking.

### AKEL EL-JABBIL
*(Lebanese Mountain Food)*
*Hearty serving of Lebanese stew in individual casserole.*
*Includes hefty chunks of lamb and beef, all lean,*
*in rich tomato sauce with freshly stewed vegetables.*
*$7.25*

### DELUXE SHEESH KEBOB ADVENTURE
*Two skewers of heavily laden Phoenician Sheesh Kebob*
*which is lean lamb chunks, sliced onions, tomatoes all garlic-sauced*
*and broiled to perfection over charcoal grill.*
*$9.75*

### HELLENIC DELIGHT
*This Greek dinner features PASTITOS*
*Finger-sized macaroni, ground lamb and beef*
*mixed with special Greek cheeses, topped with egg custard*
*and baked in many-layered temple of culinary magic.*
*$8.25*

### THE DEBKI
*Baked Kibbie - the national dish of the Lebanese.*
*Two squares of pounded lean lamb*
*and cracked wheat baked and sandwiching*
*layer of diced lamb and pignola nuts.*
*$8.75*

### SHENK-KLEESH
*Tender hefty lamb shank baked in rich tomato and onion sauce*
*and cooked to the point where the lamb literally*
*melts at your touch.*
*$8.25*

### BEDOUIN BANDIT
*Two skewers of Kefta Kebob,*
*ground lean lamb, mixed with herbs, spices,*
*broiled to keep in the juices.*
*$8.50*

### THE CAMEL GUIDE
*(SHAIKHE EL MAHSHEE)*
*For our more jaded customers who have tried almost all our menu.*
*Stuffed eggplant slices filled*
*with diced lamb and pignola nuts*
*and baked under cover of tomatoes.*
*$8.25*

### PHOENICIAN GALLEY
*Fresh Fish Fillets baked in individual Casserole*
*and smothered in a blanket of sliced strings of onion*
*and crushed sesame dressing.*
*Tantalizing gourmet.*
*$7.50*

### GRECIAN QUEEN
*(MOUSAKA)*
*Famous stuffed eggplant dish*
*features tenderly fried eggplant slices*
*covering layer of diced lamb,*
*blanketed in special egg custard sauce*
*and baked to a delightful taste.*
*$8.25*

## Philadelphia: East Philly
## MONK'S INN
## Continental $$

There's a cheery greeting boomed out by a brown-robed "monk" as you arrive; another fake friar brings a gift of cheese, bread and apples. By the time your cocktail is in hand, you're convinced you've wandered into a monastery (in fact, a former cotton mill) that has your temporal rather than your spiritual interests in mind. Dinner, to background music by Bach, Beethoven and Chopin, starts with soup (a choice of three), snails, clams or artichokes. After that there's a good entrée variety ranging from steak sautéed in an iron skillet to fresh fish. Desserts include chocolate fondue and baked Alaska flambé. The Inn is also a pleasant setting for lunch or Sunday brunch. For the latter, the prix fixe menu gives you champagne or a brunch drink followed by a salad, egg dish, fondue or quiche, coffee or tea. There's also a good selection of à la carte items, including some odd (for brunch) dishes like mussels marinière and snails. Wine is available from the keg or wine list. Keep in mind that this recommendation is for the Monk's skillful mix of kitch and conviviality rather than culinary excellence and you should share my enjoyment of the place.

MONK'S INN, 110 South Front Street, Philadelphia. Telephone: (215) 923-9557. Lunch: Monday-Saturday 11:30 am-4 pm. Dinner: Monday-Sunday 4 pm-midnight. Sunday brunch 1 pm-4 pm. Cards: AE, CB, DC, VISA. Reservations advised. Full bar service. Street parking.

Fresh Sea Trout Baked, with garniture. **8.00**

Filet de Sole Normande. **8.50**
Poached in white wine with tiny shrimps and mushrooms.

Moules Marinière. **6.50**
Mussel's in white wine and herb's.

Shrimp's Monk's Inn style, and rice Pilaf. **10.25**

Coq au Vin aux Nouilles. **8.35**
Tender chicken sauteed in a wine sauce, Garnished with baked noodles au gratin.

Coquelet Grand Mère. **8.15**
Rock Cornish hen prepared the way Grand-Mother used to.

Canard a l'orange, flambé. **9.25**
Roast duckling, flamed with brandy and escorted.

Escalope Foret Noir. **9.25**
Tender cut of veal sauteed in butter, herbs, and Black Forest mushrooms, escorted.

Steak Tartare. **9.00**
Freshly ground raw filet, garnished with a golden egg yolk, capers, onions, parsley, anchovies, Worcestershire, and ground pepper.

Entrecôte sautée a la Poele, Garnie: **11.25**
Steak sauteed in cast iron pan, cooked to your taste and garnished a la Monk's Inn.

Rognons du Chef. **7.00**
Kidney's in wine and mushroom sauce.

Veal Marengo. **7.50**
Tips of veal marinated in fresh vegetables, delicately seasoned to perfection.

Escalope Vienoise **8.25**

Quiche Lorraine. **6.95**

## Philadelphia: East Philly
# OLD ORIGINAL BOOKBINDER'S
Seafood                                        $$

The Bookbinder family opened their first seafood restaurant at this location in 1865. When the restaurant was sold in the '40s to the Taxins, the name Bookbinder was retained. Later, when the Bookbinder family opened a new restaurant on 15th Street, that restaurant also bore the Bookbinder name. Both have devoted followings. Out-of-towners seem to gravitate to this larger, better publicized location. Old Original Bookbinder's is within easy walking distance of all of the revered landmarks of Independence National Park. It is also within sight of the handsome Penn's Landing area with its passing parade of interesting cargo vessels. Across the street is a vast parking lot, not to be taken lightly in view of the city's paucity of parking spaces elsewhere. All around are the high-rent homes and apartments of Society Hill. What Bookbinder's offers tourists and neighbors alike starts with thick, sherry-fortified snapper soup and Maine lobster. It includes crabmeat, oysters, shrimp, clams and, a special treat for those who hail from inland America, just-caught fish like sole, scrod, swordfish and bluefish, all beautifully broiled with butter and lemon to accent their freshness. For Uncle Charlie, the restaurant has a meaty list of steaks and roasts featuring a Kansas sirloin steak that weighs in at a whopping 16 ounces. For the calorie-carefree, there are desserts like chocolate cake, cheesecake and strawberry shortcake, all so tall they seem designed for giants but so delicious that invariably they are devoured down to the last crumb.

OLD ORIGINAL BOOKBINDER'S, 125 Walnut Street, Philadelphia. Telephone: (215) 925-7027. Lunch: Monday-Friday 11:45-2. Dinner: Monday-Friday from 5 pm; Saturday and Sunday from 1 pm. All major credit cards. Reservations advised. Full bar service. Parking lot. Children's menu.

# Bookbinder's Specialties

## New Bedford Filet of Serod

Broiled with Tomato and Onion
in Garlic Butter.
Potato, Vegetable and Salad,
Crisp Rolls and Butter
Roquefort Cheese Dressing
.50 Extra

**10.75**

## Cold Seafood Platter

½ Lobster, Lump Crabmeat,
Fresh Jumbo Shrimp,
Cherrystone Clams and
Potato Salad

**12.50**

## Fresh Filet of Flounder

Baked with Artichokes,
Spinach, Mushrooms, with a
Cheese Stuffing

**11.50**

## Hot Seafood Platter
### Bookbinder's Specialty
### For Over 100 Years

Fresh Fish in Season, Deviled Clam,
Fried Shrimp, Crab Ball, Shrimp Salad,
Crabmeat Au Gratin
Baked Potato or French Fries,
Cole Slaw, Tartar Sauce,
"Salad"

**11.95**

# Seafood and Shellfish

### "CATCH OF THE DAY"
For Those Who Like Their Fish Made Simply with Butter and Lemon.

**NEW BEDFORD SWORDFISH** (In Season)............................10.95
**NEW BEDFORD BROILED SCROD** (A Bookbinder Favorite)......... 9.95
**NEW BEDFORD BROILED FILET OF SOLE**...........................10.50
**FRESH BROILED BLUEFISH** (Superb Local Seafood) ............... 9.95
**BROILED, IMPORTED INDIVIDUAL DOVER SOLE** .............12.95
**IMPORTED SCOTLAND FINNAN HADDIE** (A Gourmet's Delight)...10.95
**NEW BEDFORD FRIED DEEP SEA SCALLOPS** .................... 9.95
(Choice of Tartar or Cocktail Sauce.)
**NEW ENGLAND JUMBO DEVILED CLAM PLATTER**............... 8.95
**CANADIAN SILVER SMELTS** (Fried, Tartar Sauce - a Special Treat)..8.75
**FRESH COLUMBIA RIVER SALMON** (Broiled or Poached)..........12.95

# Live Maine Lobsters

The Only Good Lobster is a Live Lobster.
Rushed by Air from Maine Waters Right to Our Lobster Tanks.

**STEAMED OR BROILED 1¼ lb. MAINE LOBSTER** ................12.75
Stuffed with Shrimp or Crabmeat......................................13.50
**MEDIUM LOBSTER (2½ lbs. and over)** .............................23.95
**JUMBO LOBSTER (over 3 lbs.)** .....................................24.95
**EXTRA JUMBO MAINE LOBSTER (3½ to 4 lbs.) Serves (2)**........29.00
(When Available)
Medium or Jumbo Lobster Stuffed with Crabmeat 3.95 Extra
**BROILED SOUTH AFRICAN LOBSTER TAIL.** (1 lb. Tail) .........14.95
Sweet and Succulent, Bursting from the Shell with Drawn Butter.
**LOBSTER NEWBURG**................................................13.95
Chunks of Fresh Lobster Blended with a Sauce of Wine, Cream and Butter.
**LOBSTER STEW**...................................................13.95
Lobster Meat Cooked with Celery, Pimentos, Peppers and a Little Milk.

# Philadelphia: Center City
## ONASSIS
### Greek
$

This full-fledged Greek restaurant started as a tiny lunch-counter-type operation where the food was so great, so affordable, it was tough to get in the door at mealtime. The new Onassis is bigger, better and attractively grottolike. It provides a pleasant setting for a menu rich with lamb, phyllo pastry, eggplant, feta cheese and other delights of this sunny cuisine.

ONASSIS, 1735 Sansom Street, Philadelphia. Telephone: (215) 568-6960. Lunch: Monday-Saturday 11:30 am-4 pm. Dinner: nightly 4:30 pm-2 am. Cards: AE, MC, VISA. Reservations accepted. Full bar service. Nearby parking garage.

## Philadelphia: South Philadelphia
## PHILIP'S
## Italian

$$

Philip's is one of South Philadelphia's best-kept secrets. For 40 years, the restaurant has been hiding in a handsome old townhouse on South Broad Street. It's easy to miss unless you know to look for the canopy that leads to the upper-level entrance, or the elegant, if slightly fractured, marble Roman lady and her canine companion who stand guard at the foot of the stairs. The restaurant is pleasantly decorated with immaculately clothed tables. Waiters, on every occasion I have had to visit the restaurant, gave personal, Old World service. Lunch or dinner, Philip's offers conventional Italian dishes like veal scaloppine or beef braciola as well as some not-so-conventional ones (to non-Italians) like calves brains served sizzling deliciously in butter. Pasta dishes abound and at prices that will please an impoverished swain out to impress a dinner date. There are interesting Italian and California wines at all prices.

PHILIP'S, 1145 South Broad Street, Philadelphia. Telephone: (215) 334-0882. Hours: daily 11 am-11 pm; closed Monday. Cards: AE, DC, MC (no gratuities on credit cards). Reservations accepted. Full bar service. Street parking.

## From the Broiler

Broiled Sirloin Steak with Onions or Mushrooms . . . . 9.00
Broiled Filet Mignon with Onions or Mushrooms . . . . 9.00
Broiled Double Rack Lamb Chops (2) . . . . . . . . . . . . 9.50
Broiled Veal T-Bone with Peppers Saute . . . . . 7.50
Broiled Pork Chops (2) or a la Pizzaiola . . . . . . . . . . . 7.50
Calf's Liver with Bacon or Onions . . . . . . . . . . . . . 7.50
Half Broiled Chicken . . . . . . . . . . . . . . . . . . . 4.95
Italian Sausage with Peppers or Mushrooms Saute . . . . 5.95

## Veal Specialties

Veal Scallopine
    with Marsala Wine and Mushrooms . . . . . . 5.75
    with Peppers and Mushrooms, Rosso . . . . 5.75
    a la Cacciatore . . . . . . . . . . . . . . . . 5.95
    Sorrento a la Marinara . . . . . . . . . . . . 5.95
    Picante (Lemon and Butter) . . . . . . . . . 5.75
    a la Romana (Mozzarella, Salami, Anchovies
      in Wine Sauce) . . . . . . . . . . . . . . . 6.95
    Saltimbocca (Prosciutto and Mozzarella
      in Wine Sauce) . . . . . . . . . . . . . . . 6.95
Veal Rollatini with Peppers and Mushrooms, Rosso
  or Marsala Wine . . . . . . . . . . . . . . . . 6.95
Veal Cutlet Milanese, French Fried Potatoes . . . . . 4.95
Veal Cutlet a la Parmigiana, French Fried Potatoes . . 5.50

## Philip's Favorites

Chicken Livers a la Veneziana . . . . . . . . . . . . . . . 5.50
Boneless Breast of Capon Parmigiana, French Fries . . . . 5.50
Italian Sausage Parmigiana or a la Cacciatore . . . . . . . 5.95
Chicken a la Cacciatore, Bianco or Rosso . . . . . . . . . 6.95
Calves Brains au Gratin en Casserole . . . . . . . . . . . 5.95
Trippa a la Romana . . . . . . . . . . . . . . . . . . . . 5.50
Sweetbreads Florentine . . . . . . . . . . . . . . . . . 6.95
Beef Braciola a la Napolitana . . . . . . . . . . . . . . . 6.95
Sliced Beef Tenderloin with Marsala Wine and Mushrooms . 8.50
Veal Scallopine alla Florentina . . . . . . . . . . . . . . 6.95

## From the Sea

Clams Casino . . . . . . . . . 3.95    Shrimp Marinara . . . 6.50
Clams Areganata . . . . . . . 3.50    Calamai a la Philip's . 5.95
Shrimp Con Risotto a la Philip's . 6.95    Flounder Florentina . 5.95
Mussels fra Diavolo, Rosso or Bianco . . . . . . . . . . . . 3.75
Shrimp Marinara with Peppers and Mushrooms . . . . . . . 6.95
Broiled South African Lobster Tails, Drawn Butter . . . . . 9.00
Fried Canadian Smelts, Tartar Sauce . . . . . . . . . . . . 4.95

## Pasta

Spaghetti with either Tomato, Marinara or Butter Sauce . . . 3.50
with Clams, Rosso or Bianco    4.50     with Shrimp . . . . . 4.95
with Chicken Liver . . . . . . 4.50     with Sausage . . . . . 4.95
with Anchovies Aglio e Olio . . 4.95     a la Caruso, Mushrooms
with Ravioli . . . . . . . . . 3.95     and Chicken Livers 4.95
Ravioli with either Tomato, Marinara or Butter Sauce . . . . 3.95

## Philadelphia: Center City
## PICCOLO PADRE
## Italian

**$$$**

The big, brash sign outside Piccolo Padre may lead you to think you're making a mistake. A sign like that could only lead to a bar, a luncheonette or a pizza parlor, no? The sign is largely deceiving. Yes, there's a bar just inside the door, but there's a wood-paneled dining room beyond that's a happy blaze of red, white and green linens. And a northern Italian menu that shows imagination and talent. Expect excellent mussels, homemade pasta, interesting meat courses like roast baby lamb and veal with lemon. Among the attractive dessert choices is a homemade cake of many layers topped with buttery, citron-flecked frosting. There's a wine list that matches up nicely with the food.

PICCOLO PADRE, 303 South 11th Street, Philadelphia. Telephone: (215) 925-8192. Hours: dinner only, Tuesday-Saturday from 5 pm. Cards: AE, DC, MC, VISA. Reservations suggested. Full bar service. Street parking.

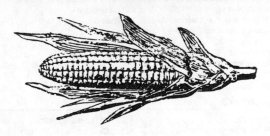

## Philadelphia: Center City
## THE RESTAURANT
International                                    $

Do you believe budding restaurant talent should be en-
couraged? Do you believe it enough to gamble $6.95 on
it? Answer yes and you're a candidate for one of The
Restaurant's white-clothed tables. Insist on consistency,
however, and you'll spend your cash somewhere the staff
doesn't change with a flip of the calendar page. The Restaurant, you see, is an on-the-job training ground for a prac-
tical and much-applauded local restaurant school. The students, directed by professionals, pay to work as they learn,
rotating jobs. Some of the best restaurant food in town, I
might add, is being prepared these days by early Restaurant
School grads. Initially, The Restaurant charged the same
prices as places run by pros, but in recent years, the
students have been challenged to produce a full meal selling
for $6.95 exclusive of dessert and wine. Although you
don't get a guarantee of exquisite food, you can be reason-
ably sure the meal will be interesting and carefully prepared. Red and white wines are available to accompany the
food.

THE RESTAURANT, 2129 Walnut Street, Philadelphia.
Telephone: (215) 561-3649. Hours: dinner only, Tuesday-
Friday 5:30-9:30 pm; Saturday 5:30-10 pm. Cards: AE,
MC, VISA. Reservations advised. Wine only. Street parking.

## Philadelphia: Center City
## RESTAURANT MAUREEN
French                                                        **$$**

Maureen is a widely traveled, food-knowledgeable young woman who is half the reason this small, caring French restaurant receives applause from food critics. It is Maureen who greets and seats you, explains the menu and helps you find a wine from the small but attractive selection she strives to keep moderately priced. Equal partner in the restaurant's success, however, is husband Stephen Horn, a chef whose approach to French food is described by his wife as "slightly iconoclastic." A popular Horn creation is duckling with fresh strawberry sauce. Tournedos of beef crowned with crabmeat and sauced with Béarnaise is another specialty in the nouvelle cuisine vein chef Horn is currently mining. For less adventurous diners, there is sirloin sautéed and served with fresh mushrooms or simply elegant smoked salmon, an appetizer that arrives with a pony of icy Stolichnaya vodka. Previous owners decorated the restaurant in brassy blue vinyl but the nightclubby flash is being replaced gradually and may well have vanished by the time you read this.

RESTAURANT MAUREEN, 11 South 21st Street, Philadelphia. Telephone: (215) 561-3542. Hours: Tuesday-Saturday 5:30 pm-10 pm. Cards: AE, DC, MC, VISA. Reservations advised. Full bar service. Nearby parking lot and garages.

Entrecôte   12.95

marinated Sirloin steak sautéed and served in the
Chef's special sauce with fresh mushrooms.

Tournedos Royale  14.50

petite filets of beef sautéed with shallots, glazed in
red wine, crowned with crabmeat and served with
sauce bearnaise.

Escalopes de Veau Maureen  11.50

slices of natured Veal sautéed with shallots and
served with a special lemon sauce with fresh Mushrooms.

Médaillons de Veau au Bec Rouge  14.50

médaillons of natured veal sautéed and served on
a bed of Lobster, shrimp and crab ~ served
with sauce St. Milo.

Canard aux Fraises  11.50

roast duckling served with a sauce of fresh Strawberries

Cassolette d'ecrevisses Marinière  12.95

lobster ~ shrimp and crab sautéed and served
in a light white wine sauce.

Truites Farci aux Amandes  10.50

boneless brook Trout baked in white wine
stuffed with crab and served Almandine.

Homard en Feuilletage à Lyon  15.50

south african lobster tail removed from the shell,
served with a light stuffing of lobster and dill
seasoning, wrapped in the Chef's own puff pastry.

## Philadelphia: Center City
## RIPPLEMYER'S CAFÉ VIENNA
Austrian/Greek/Italian                    **$$**

Faux marble tabletops rest on heavy iron pedestals. Frosted glass lights dangle over each table. There's the feeling here that you've wandered into a Victorian conservatory and that a mustachioed butler awaits your command behind the massive oak server. Ripplemyer's used to be a glorified ice cream parlour says new owner Irvin Gelber. It has taken months, he reports, but he's finally managed to exorcise that ghost and give the place a new identity as a serious restaurant. Gelber, who mans the Ripplemyer kitchen, spent several years in Vienna and he brings his enthusiasm for the food of that part of the world to his cooking. Case in point, the menu's three schnitzels: rahm (in heavy cream with mushrooms), paprika (with sour cream paprika sauce) and wiener (veiled in egg and crumbs then sizzled in butter). Gelber has a Greek background also, and it shows in the menu's stuffed grape leaves, Greek salad and flounder in a classic lemon sauce. His interest in Italy is represented by fettuccine Alfredo and fettuccine cinque terre (with tomato, eggplant, olives and herbs). Some of the best freelance bakers in the city concoct Ripplemyer's cakes du jour. The dessert menu also includes frozen yogurt and ice cream for those who can't quite forget they once came here for a double dip of butter pecan.

**RIPPLEMYER'S CAFÉ VIENNA, 1300 Pine Street, Phila-delphia. Telephone: (212) 46-0777. Hours: Tuesday-Sunday, lunch from noon; dinner from 5:30. No cards. Reservations advised. No alcoholic beverages; bring your own wine. Street parking.**

Onion Soup .. 1.75   Soup du jour .. 1.75   Quiche du
jour .. 1.75 - 2.25   Stuffed Grape Leaves .. 1.95
House Salad .. 1.25   Fresh Fruit in season .. 1.25


Greek "peasant" Salad .. 3.95   Curried Chicken
Salad .. 3.95   Salad Nicoise .. 4.25   Chef's
Salad Bowl .. 4.25


## PASTA

Fettuccine Cinque Terre ..tomato/eggplant/          4.50
   olives/herbs sauce
Fettuccine Alfredo .. heavy cream/butter/           4.75
   parmesan cheese sauce

## FISH

Flounder Theodore .. fillet in lemon/butter/        7.25
   wine/mushroom sauce
Flounder Mykonos .. fillet in classic Greek         7.25
   lemon/olive oil/oregano sauce

## CHICKEN

Chicken Kapama .. breast of chicken in a            6.50
   tomato sauce accented with cinnamon
Chicken Paprikas .. breast of chicken baked         6.75
   in sour cream/onions/peppers/paprika
Wiener Backhendl .. breast of chicken marinated 6.75
   in lemon, lightly dipped in flour, egg
   and bread crumbs ... sauteed

## VEAL

Rahmschnitzel .. scallop of veal in heavy           7.50
   cream and mushrooms
Paprikaschnitzel .. scallop of veal in              7.50
   paprika sauce finished with sour cream
Wiener Schnitzel .. scallop of veal lightly         7.50
   dipped in flour, egg and bread crumbs
   ... sauteed


Cakes du jour .. 1.75   Whipped Frozen Yogurt .. 1.50
Louis Sherry Ice Cream .. 1.50   Fresh Fruit in
season .. 1.25   Coffee ...50   Espresso .. .95   Cafe
au lait .. 1.00   Capuccino .. 1.25   Teas .. .50
   Sparkling Cider .. 1.00   Perrier Water .. 1.00

101

## RISTORANTE DA GAETANO
Italian

**$$$**

Ines is mildly annoyed. A young restaurant critic has called her homemade pasta "too thin." Gaetano, her husband, smiles. "It is too thin," he says teasingly. "It would be thicker in some Italian restaurants ... but not in Italian homes." And that is what Gaetano gives you, the cooking of an elegant northern Italian home kitchen served in a stylish, brick-walled restaurant setting. Ines and Gaetano own and operate the restaurant, rarely relinquishing the role of host or hostess to hired help. Ines makes the pasta, mountains of it, then rushes back to their home nearby to dress elegantly for the dinner crowd. The two flatter and pamper familiar faces shamelessly. That's splendid when it happens to you but it can be tough on onlookers and, over the years, I've heard comments from a handful of disgruntled diners who felt left out. (I've also heard from many more who consider the restaurant the best of its kind in the States.) Portions are kept small to let you order a full, well-orchestrated Italian feast without forcing you to let out another notch in your Gucci belt. Budget watchers should be forewarned that courses have a way of adding up at check time. You get what you pay for, however. The pasta is as tender as whispered sweet nothings and sauces can be as creamy and smooth as Ines' flattery. Specialties of the house include an osso buco that will make you understand all the fuss made about this humble dish based on shin bones and their marrow. Any veal dish is a delight. Try the piccata di vitello al limone if you like your veal paper-thin, buttery and lightly kissed with lemon. Order cocktails and Ines might slip over to your table bearing slices of her special pastry ribboned with fine bands of fennel-flavored sausage. Gaetano's Italian wine list makes the best of Pennsylvania's annoyingly restrictive state store system. Recently, the restaurant added an upper-level gallery that lets you enjoy the current exhibit while you sip your Campari and soda.

RISTORANTE DA GAETANO, 727 Walnut Street, Philadelphia. Telephone: (215) 922-3771. Lunch: Tuesday-Friday 11:30 am-2 pm. Dinner: Tuesday-Friday 6 pm-9:30 pm; Saturday dinner to 10 pm; closed Sunday and Monday. Cards: AE, DC, VISA. Reservations advised. Full bar service. Parking in nearby lot.

## Philadelphia: Center City
## RISTORANTE IL GALLO NERO
## Italian                                      $$

Il Gallo Nero is center city's stylish new Italian dining spot. A rooster etched on the front window, white walls, white linens and bright, poster-color graphics all help make this a chic setting for well-dressed folks in pursuit of the ultimate in northern Italian cuisine. The list of food offerings is long and especially interesting in the pasta category where one finds temptations ranging from pappardelle, the wide yellow noodles traditionally served with a wild hare sauce, to small stuffed, doughnutlike tortellini.

RISTORANTE IL GALLO NERO, 254 South 15th Street, Philadelphia. Telephone: (215) 546-8065. Lunch: Monday-Friday from 11:30 am. Dinner: Monday-Saturday from 5 pm; closed Sunday. Cards: AE, DC, MC, VISA. Reservations advised. Full bar service. Nearby parking lot.

# Philadelphia: Riverfront
## RIVERFRONT
International $$

By day, there's a constantly changing pattern of river traffic to watch. By night, there are Camden's twinkling lights, strung out like diamonds-by-the-yard against the black satin of the Delaware River. The Riverfront has one of the city's best commuter restaurant locations, easily reached by car from most parts of town and with parking space to spare. It also has a fascinating history. Once a fire gutted the place. In another early incarnation, a chunk of supporting pier tumbled into the river. Three owners have had to yell "uncle." The fourth, and current, has turned this Titanic of a loser into a smooth sailing operation. Lee Tabas (of Downingtown Inn fame) has given the place a no-nonsense name and a promising new identity. Not only is the Riverfront a successful restaurant, it's a thriving dinner theater as well. With *Gypsy, Guys and Dolls* or whatever the current attraction, you get a bountiful buffet that includes roast beef, seafood (in season, clams and oysters are available on the half shell) homebaked breads and freshly baked desserts. If you're here for the view and the food and not the show, there's an excellent salad buffet, lots of fresh seafood choices, plus grilled steaks, roasts and a few elegant veal and poultry dishes. A large, nicely balanced lunch menu offers salads, sandwiches, eggs and a selection of hot luncheon platters. There's always broiled fish, really fresh and piping hot. Lunchtime service recognizes most diners' lunchtime limitations.

RIVERFRONT RESTAURANT AND DINNER THEATRE, on the Delaware River, north of Spring Garden Street at Poplar, Philadelphia. Telephone: (215) 925-7000. Lunch: Tuesday-Saturday 11:30-2:30. Dinner: Tuesday-Friday 6-10; Saturday 5:30-9; Sunday 3-9. Cards: AE, DC, MC, VISA. Reservations advised. Full bar service. Free parking.

## Riverfront Specialties

**BROILED HALF NEW JERSEY SPRING CHICKEN** . . . . . . . . . . . . . . . . . . . . . . . . . . . . . . . . . . . . . . . 7.95
Delicately seasoned for added flavor and goodness

**STUFFED BONELESS BREAST OF CAPON "Garni"** . . . . . . . . . . . . . . . . . . . . . . . . . . . . . . . . . . . 8.95
Boneless breast of capon with savory dressing of bread and wild rice, with a delicate
chicken sauce with fresh mushrooms, green pepper, and red pimentos

**ROAST DUCKLING A'L'ORANGE, Sauce Bigarade** . . . . . . . . . . . . . . . . . . . . . . . . . . . . . . . . . . . 8.95
Rubbed with crushed spices and then roasted to perfection; served with our special
orange sauce and a timbale of wild rice

**MEDAILLONS DE VEAU PARISIENNE** . . . . . . . . . . . . . . . . . . . . . . . . . . . . . . . . . . . . . . . . . . . . . . 9.95
Milk-fed veal, dipped in egg, sautéed, garnished with asparagus

**BROILED SPRING LAMB CHOPS** . . . . . . . . . . . . . . . . . . . . . . . . . . . . . . . . . . . . . . . . . . . . . . . 13.95
Two double rib broiled to perfection, served with mint jelly

**VEAL FLORENTINE** . . . . . . . . . . . . . . . . . . . . . . . . . . . . . . . . . . . . . . . . . . . . . . . . . . . . . . . . . . 12.96
Thick cut milk fat veal chops, sautéed in butter and topped with delicate fresh
mushroom sauce, garnished with tomato provencial

**ROAST U.S.D.A. PRIME RIBS OF BLEU RIBBON BEEF, AU JUS** . . . . . . . . . . . . . . . . . . . . . . 11.95
From our aging locker comes the finest cut of juicy beef

**CHARCOAL BROILED U.S.D.A. PRIME NEW YORK SIRLOIN STEAK** . . . . . . . . . . . . . . . . . . . 14.95
A thick, prime cut, ember-broiled to your preference and served with
mushroom caps and fried onion rings

**CHARCOAL BROILED U.S.D.A. PRIME FILET MIGNON** . . . . . . . . . . . . . . . . . . . . . . . . . . . . . 14.95
The heart of prime tenderloin, broiled to perfection and served with fresh
mushroom caps and fried onion rings

## Seafood and Shellfish

**FRESH BABY FLOUNDER FILET "MEUNIERE"** . . . . . . . . . . . . . . . . . . . . . . . . . . . . . . . . . . . . 9.95
Delicately sautéed in butter
Broiled stuffed with Fresh Lump Crabmeat . . . . . . . . . . . . . . . . . . . . . . . . . . . . . . . . . . . . . . . 13.95

**BAKED CRABMEAT IMPERIAL** . . . . . . . . . . . . . . . . . . . . . . . . . . . . . . . . . . . . . . . . . . . . . . . . 10.95
Fresh lump crabmeat, baked in a shell, laced with sherry and a tasty cream sauce
and glazed with buttered bread crumbs

**POACHED SALMON STEAK AU "CHAMPAGNE" "Air Shipped from Alaska"** . . . . . . . . . . . . . . 10.45
Fresh salmon in a creamy sauce, seasoned with champagne

**DOVER SOLE "BELLE MEUNIERE" "Imported from England"** . . . . . . . . . . . . . . . . . . . . . . . . . 11.95
Fresh sole sautéed and covered with sizzling almond butter

**BROILED GENUINE SOUTH AFRICAN LOBSTER TAILS** . . . . . . . . . . . . . . . . . . . . . . . . . . . . 14.95
Broiled with New England style seasoning; served with warm butter

**RIVERFRONT SEAFOOD COMBINATION** . . . . . . . . . . . . . . . . . . . . . . . . . . . . . . . . . . . . . . . . 15.95
South African lobster tail, fried jumbo Caribbean shrimp and plump scallops
. . . all from the world of the deep

**PORT O' CALL COMBINATION** . . . . . . . . . . . . . . . . . . . . . . . . . . . . . . . . . . . . . . . . . . . . . . . . 15.95
Prime filet mignon teamed with South African lobster tail

**BROILED MAINE LOBSTER, live from our tank, 2 lbs. "plus"** . . . . . . . . . . . . . . . . . . . . . . Price
Served with drawn butter and fresh lemon;          According to
or STUFFED OVERFLOWING WITH LUMP CRABMEAT . . . . . . . . . . . . . . . . . . . . . . Market

**"SALAD ONLY" from the Salad Bar (without a dinner entree)** . . . . . . . . . . 6.95

## Philadelphia: Chinatown
## RIVERSIDE CHINESE RESTAURANT
## Chinese $

How does a good new Chinatown restaurant call attention to itself in the Chinese puzzle of good old restaurants that proliferate in the area? The landlocked Riverside does it with a name that's unlike any of its neighbors' and a separate dim sum menu. Dim sum are the Chinese equivalent of what the French might call hors d'oeuvre, and the English, "savouries." The term covers a wide variety of what we'd call snacks or munchies, ranging from salty, savory fried pastries to delicate steamed dumplings with paper-thin dough wrappings and finely minced fillings. The dim sum vary but on one visit we enjoyed small spring rolls with extremely crisp coatings; steamed, slightly chewy mounds of dough powdered with flour and filled with coconut and peanuts; triangular taro-paste fried pastries; chewy beef meatballs flavored with watercress and exquisite steamed shrimp dumplings. As one plate is emptied, your waiter or waitress arrives with another. The Riverside's regular menu offers the usual pick-from-the-column specials, plus many other popular Chinese dishes. Spicy Szechwan and Hunan preparations are listed in red with asterisks.

RIVERSIDE CHINESE RESTAURANT, 234 North Ninth Street, Philadelphia. Telephone: (215) 923-4410. Hours: daily from 10:30 am. Cards: MC, VISA. No reservations. No alcoholic beverages. Pay parking across the street.

# Our Chef's Suggestions

**House Wor Bar**    6.25

A delightful blend of lobster, shrimp, slices of chicken and Chinese Bar-B-Q pork, with hearts of Chinese vegetables, mushroom, waterchestnut and bamboo shoot. Served on a sizzling platter.

**\*Shrimp Szechuan Style**    5.25

A very spicy dish. For those who like it hot! Cooked in real hot pepper sauce, flavored with garlic and ginger.

**Moo Shu Pork**    4.25

Shredded pork julianned with yellow lilies and Chinese vegetable. Served with pancakes.

**Lychee Duck**    5.75

Chinese barbecued duck to crisp brown, blended with sweet and pungent sauce, subtly flavored with lichees.

**\*Lamb Wu Nan Style**    5.25

Slices of tender lamb meat, sauteed in a rich brown sauce topped with heads of green scallion in a tangy hot pepper sauce.

**Riverside Treasure**    6.50

Tender cubes of beef, lobster chunks, shrimps, slices of B-B-Q pork, mushroom and snow peas cooked with black bean sauce and a mere suspicion of garlic. For educated palates.

**Sum Kip Tai**    4.95

Fine cut of    cubes of chicken, slices of Bar-B-Q roast duck and fresh shrimp, blended deliciously with pineapple, snow peas and mushrooms.

**Sea Food Combination**    7.25

A savory combination of lobster chunks, crab meat, shrimp, squid and fish ball, blended with imported golden baby corn, straw mushrooms and tender slices of bamboo shoot in our chef's secret sauce.

**Steamed Clams**    4.50

For the seafood lovers. Here is a platter of steamed cherry stone clams, blended in a rich black bean and garlic sauce with a touch of a tangy hot pepper sauce.

**Lemon Chicken**    4.75

Boneless breast chicken, lightly crusted in egg batter and sauteed. Served in a mild lemon sauce, topped with crusted almonds.

**\*Kung Po Chicken**    4.25

A well known spicy Mandarin dish, originated from the Ching Dynasty. Its main ingredients are simple: Diced cut of chicken breast, cashew nut and hot pepper. But, My, What a Taste.

**Peking Spare Ribs**    4.25

Marinated fresh spareribs with special spices, flavored with pickled onions in a zestful creamy sugar and vinegar sauce.

**Yang Chow Fried Rice**    3.75

Special fried rice with shrimp, chicken and pork in assorted beans.

**Pa Chen Duck**    7.95

An authentic Chinese favorite. Half boneless braised duck, crowned with a succulent combination of fresh shrimps, squid, slices of ham, Bar-B-Q pork, shrimp balls, mushrooms, snow peapods and hearts of Chinese green vegetable.

**\*Chiang Pao Beef**    4.75

Diced cut of beef, green pepper and preserved turnip, cooked in a Mandarin manner and flavored with a mashed bean sauce. A spicy dish.

**\*Crab Meat Szechuan Style**    6.75

Deep fried crab meat sauteed in our hot spicy sauce.

## Philadelphia: Center City
## RUSSELL'S
## International

**$$**

Russell's is very much a low-key, comfortable neighborhood restaurant, yet because of its location—convenient to department stores, theaters and hotels—it attracts lots of outsiders too. All are welcome in this charmingly converted corner store with its multi-paned windows, handmade café curtains and matching cushions. The menu, inked on a brown-paper lunch bag, changes frequently. On a recent visit, the bag "held" hot and hearty homemade vegetable soup, artistically arranged salads, garlic-sauced shrimp and almond-sauced chicken. Cooking is to order in a kitchen that's in full view of the dining room. Entrée prices are modest and include soup or salad and vegetable. There's no liquor license so you keep the bill down even lower by bringing your own wine. Desserts get their fair share of attention from the kitchen. Sampled and rated excellent were the whipped cream-lavished Black Forest cake and a fluffy, delicate pie flavored with peanut liqueur.

RUSSELL'S, 1700 Lombard Street, Philadelphia. Telephone: (215) 735-8070. Lunch: Tuesday-Friday 11-2. Dinner: Tuesday-Thursday 5-10; Friday and Saturday 5:30-11. Sunday brunch 11 am-3 pm. Cards: MC, VISA. Reservations advised. No alcoholic beverages; bring your own wine. Street parking.

## Philadelphia: Center City
## SANSOM STREET OYSTER HOUSE
Seafood                                                   $

It didn't take long for word to get around that this newest
of Philadelphia's old-fashioned oyster houses is following in
the city's tradition of serving fresh fish and shellfish without frills. Sansom House has bare floors, bare tables and
walls barely embellished with a collection of oyster plates,
some antique. All of the clams and oysters are opened on
the premises and—a nice note—they're sold individually.
Prices vary. A single cherrystone clam costs 30 cents. A
littleneck is 35 cents; for the same price you get a freshly
opened, sea-salty oyster. For 50 cents, get one of the
whopping-big, box oysters. Buy six of any one variety or
size and save from five to 15 cents. In addition to the raw
delights of the oyster bar, the restaurant cooks up oyster
and clam stews (and a stew that combines both deliciously),
fried fish and shellfish platters and daily broiled fresh fish
specials. Desserts are plain and homespun—the kind grand-
mother made. The wine list might not thrill you but then
they didn't call this the Sansom Street Wine House did
they?

SANSOM STREET OYSTER HOUSE, 1516 Sansom Street,
Philadelphia. Telephone: (215) 567-7683. Lunch: Monday-
Saturday 11-3. Dinner: Monday-Thursday 3-8; Friday and
Saturday to 9. Closed Sunday. No cards. No reservations.
Full bar service. Nearby parking garage.

## Appetizers

| | |
|---|---|
| Chilled Tomato Juice | .50 |
| Shrimp Cocktail | 2.95 |
| Crabmeat Cocktail | 4.25 |
| Broiled Oysters 3 for | 2.25 |

## Soups & Stews

| Soups | Cup | Bowl |
|---|---|---|
| Clam Chowder | .60 | 1.10 |
| Snapper | .75 | 1.40 |

| Stews | Small | Large |
|---|---|---|
| Oyster | 1.55 | 2.95 |
| Minced Clam | 1.55 | 2.95 |
| Box Oyster | 4.00 | |
| Box Clam | 3.50 | |
| Combination Stew | 4.25 | |

With cream, .30 extra

## From The Oyster Bar

| | |
|---|---|
| Cherrystone Clams | .30 ea. |
| 6 for | 1.75 |
| Little Neck Clams | .35 ea. |
| 6 for | 2.00 |
| Box Oysters | .60 ea. |
| 6 for | 2.85 |
| Half Shell Oysters | .35 ea. |
| 6 for | 2.00 |

## Cold Platter Favorites

| | |
|---|---|
| Tuna Salad | 4.25 |
| Shrimp Salad | 4.95 |
| Chicken Salad | 4.25 |
| Mixed Seafood Platter | 6.95 |
| Whole Cold Shrimp Platter | 7.95 |
| Backfin Crabmeat Platter | 7.95 |

## Steamed Specialties

| | |
|---|---|
| Clams | 3.95 |
| Shrimp * | 7.95 |

## Prime Meats *

| | |
|---|---|
| Chopped Sirloin Steak | 4.75 |
| Open Face Steak Sandwich | 5.95 |

### SANSOM ST. OYSTER HOUSE

1516 SANSOM STREET
LO7-7683

*Our clams & oysters are opened on the premises.*

## Desserts

| | |
|---|---|
| Ice Cream | .60 |
| Creamy Cheese Cake | 1.05 |
| Chocolate Pudding | .65 |
| Homemade Bread Pudding | .60 |
| Melon in Season | .75 |
| Rice Pudding | .65 |
| Fruit Pie | .65 |
| Pecan Pie | .90 |

## Dinner Platters *

| | |
|---|---|
| Fried Oysters | 4.25 |
| Devil Crab | 5.50 |
| Fried Shrimp | 5.50 |
| Devil Clam | 3.95 |
| Fried Scallops | 5.75 |
| Fried Sole | 4.95 |
| Fried Seafood Combination | 6.50 |

| | |
|---|---|
| Baked Crab Imperial | 8.25 |
| Flounder Stuffed with Crabmeat | 8.75 |
| Oyster Pan Roast | 4.95 |

*Broiled Favorites*

| | |
|---|---|
| Flounder | 6.25 |
| Bluefish | 5.25 |
| Steak Cod | 4.95 |

*All platters include French Bread & Butter, French Fried Potatoes, and Vegetable du Jour.*

## SHIPPEN'S BAR & RESTAURANT
Continental                                    **$$**

There aren't many in-town restaurants that can offer a brunch setting as attractive as Shippen's mirrored, brick-walled garden. Moreover, when the sun isn't filtering through the bright yellow awning you can enjoy the garden view from a table inside. By night, Shippen's bar becomes the fashionable meeting place for this neighborhood of young professionals. Beyond the bar, the garden-side dining room provides the low lighting and appropriate music for intimate dining. The restaurant recently revised its menu. The ambitious new list emphasizes French and Italian fare. Among the former are snails sautéed in garlic butter with hazlenuts and tournedos of beef with green peppercorns. There is always a pasta of the day as well as daily specials of chicken and fish. Other specials include bouillabaisse made with fresh fish, shrimp and lobster tails and steak prepared Russian style with vodka, sour cream and caviar.

SHIPPEN'S BAR & RESTAURANT, 701 South Fourth Street, Philadelphia. Telephone: (215) 925-2325. Lunch: Saturday 12-3. Dinner: Wednesday-Saturday 5-midnight; Sunday 5-11. Sunday brunch 12-3. Closed Monday and Tuesday. All major credit cards. Reservations advised. Full bar service. Street parking. Live music.

## SALADS

HEARTS OF PALM — 4.00

SPINACH SALAD — 3.75
  cream cheese & garlic dressing

SALADE DU JARDIN — 3.00
  assorted lettuce with vinaigrette dressing

## ENTREES

CARRÉ D'AGNEAU — 13.75
  Rack of lamb broiled with Dijon mustard seasoned with
  bread crumbs, topped with Port wine sauce

BROILED SIRLOIN — 11.75

ENTRECOTE À LA SHIPPENS — 12.50
  Prime surloin topped with onions, mushrooms, asparagus,
  flavored with garlic & Marsala wine

FILET MIGNON DU CHEF — 13.00
  broiled & topped with garlic butter, chopped ham & spices

TOURNEDOS AU POIVRE VERT — 13.00
  filet mignon topped with green peppercorn sauce

ESCALOPE DE VEAU NORMANDE — 11.50
  served in cream sauce flavored with Calvados & Dijon
  mustard, with mussels & mushrooms

VEAL PICCATINA — 10.50
  sauteed in butter & lemon juice

VEAL CAPRICCIOSA — 11.50
  served with a succulent mixture of chopped capers, olives,
  & parsley, topped with proscuitto & cheese

CAPON DU CONTINENT — 9.00
  sauteed with madeira wine & mushrooms

CAPON DU JOUR

FISH DU JOUR

PASTA DU JOUR

## Philadelphia: East Philly
## SILVER CELLAR
Ukranian/Fondue                                    $$

Yulana Baluch, who with her architect husband owns the
Silver Cellar, says she designed the candlelit hideaway as "a
place with lots of atmosphere for lovers of all ages." The
Queen Village establishment includes a basement-level cave
lined with cozy high-backed booths and an adjoining multi-
story lounge and disco that's amply mirrored for the nar-
cissist set. The menu is divided three ways, into fondues,
daily specialties and substantial dishes from the Ukraine
(where the model-pretty Yulana was born 34 years ago).
The fondues are fun, the Ukranian dishes a little heavy and
the specialties get points for trying.

SILVER CELLAR, 205 Bainbridge, Philadelphia. Tele-
phone: (215) 922-4152. Hours: Wednesday-Saturday 6
pm-11 pm. Cards: AE, DC, MC, VISA. Reservations ad-
vised. Full bar service. Street parking.

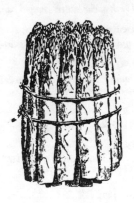

## Philadelphia: East Philly
## THE SPAGHETTI FACTORY
Italian $

The vegetables in the minestrone are from the Ninth Street market. The rum cake, bread and cannoli are South Philly products, too. What makes this little Italian restaurant different from a half-dozen or so similar eateries? The others are all in Philadelphia's Italian heartland. The Spaghetti Factory is above South Street, in a neighborhood more like Soho than Naples. Can success come to a pasta palace on the wrong side of Little Italy? It has. In the three years since the doors opened (on July 4), business has been booming. What was once an old-fashioned dry goods store, complete with stamped-tin ceiling, has been stripped down to bare brick walls and shining floors. Decor consists largely of a part new, part old neon sign that spells out "spaghetti" across the dining room wall. The real attraction here is the price. It's possible, even with inflation, for two to eat to seam-splitting satisfaction for under $20. The menu features pasta, of course, but you'll also find dishes like shrimp "scampi," chicken livers on garlic toast, mussels in red or white sauces and super salads. If you can save space for dessert, try the rum cake. Owner Barry Gomer says that he's fighting to keep his wine prices in line with those of the food.

THE SPAGHETTI FACTORY, 528 South Fifth Street, Philadelphia. Telephone: (215) 922-9577. Lunch: daily 11-2:30. Dinner: from 5:30 except Sunday from 4:30. Closed Tuesday. Cards: AE, DC, MC, VISA. Reservations accepted. Full bar service. Street parking.

## Philadelphia: East Philly
## SIVA'S
## Indian

**$$**

Saffron-tinted linens cover the tables; wicker art nouveau lamps cast soft light over those tables. At interesting intervals along the cool white walls are paneled collages with hundreds of tiny mirrored "eyes" winking back at the candlelight. Does that sound like any Indian restaurant you've seen in Philadelphia? It shouldn't. Siva's is new, elegant and—best news of all—dedicated to bringing this area a different brand of Indian food. Siva's accent is northern Indian. The chef was flown here from that part of the world. The glass-enclosed kitchen holds a clay tandoor oven from which all manner of delectable barbecued meats and even breads emerge. Spices for these and other dishes are custom blended and some recipes contain well over a dozen different seasonings. Cloves, cumin, coriander, cinnamon, cardamom, allspice, saffron and fenugreek all appear with fair frequency. The menu is a booklike affair of many pages and lists appetizers, breads, tandoor specialties, other Indian entrées, soups, vegetables and desserts. There's something exciting for everyone in almost every category. Vegetarian appetizer fritters are good enough to inspire a meat boycott. Until you taste the yogurt-marinated lamb or chicken, that is. The breads? There's puffy puri, Siva's chicken-stuffed naan, spicy, oniony kulcha. Freshly made chutneys (my favorite is mint) serve as dips for fritters or breads. Indian desserts are in direct contrast to most other dishes in their often extraordinary blandness.

SIVA'S, 34 South Front Street, Philadelphia. Telephone: (215) 925-2700. Lunch: Tuesday-Friday noon-2 pm. Dinner: Tuesday-Friday 5:30-10:30 pm; Saturday 5:30-11:30 pm; Sunday 4-10 pm. Closed Monday. Cards: AE, CB, DC, MC, VISA. Reservations accepted. Full bar service. Street parking.

# SIFARISH-E-KHAS
Our Chef's Recommendations

### SPECIAL TANDOORI MIX     12.00
Tandoori Chicken, Boti Kebab, Seekh Kebab, Chicken Tikka, Mattar Pillaw, Dal, Sabzi Kofta and Naan

### SPECIAL VEGETARIAN·THALI     8.50
Three varieties of vegetables (Bengan Bhurta, Dal, and Sabzi Kofta), Samosa, Pillaw, Raita, Puri, and Dessert.

# SAMUNDER SE
Seafood Delicacies

### PRAWN·MIRCH·MASALA     9.00
King-size shrimps cooked with green peppers, tomatoes and onions

### PRAWN·BHUNA     9.00
Prawns submerged in a puree of fresh green herbs and blended with sauteed onions and fresh mint

### FISH·MASALA     8.00
Fish cooked with coconut, herbs and spices.

# TANDOOR SE
From our special clay oven — THE TANDOOR
Introduction to TANDOORI CHARCOAL BARBEQUES

### TANDOORI·CHICKEN     4.75    8.50
Spring chicken marinated in yoghurt and freshly ground spices roasted in the charcoal clay oven

### RESHAMI·KEBAB     7.00
Tender chicken morsels very lightly spiced and Tandoori-cooked

### CHICKEN·TIKKA     7.00
Marinated boneless chicken cubes roasted in the Tandoor

### BOTI·KEBAB     7.50
Tender morsels of lamb on skewers and roasted to perfection in the Tandoor

### SEEKH·KEBAB     7.50
Minced lamb mixed with onions and herbs, roasted on skewers

### TANDOORI·PRAWNS     11.00
Prawns marinated in special sauce and herbs, roasted on skewers — Tender and delicious.

### SHEESH·KEBAB·MAGHLAI     8.00
Ground filet of beef blended with a special mixture of spices and herbs — barbecued on skewers over charcoal in the "Tandoor."

### SHEESH·KEBAB·KABLI     9.00
Diced filet of beef marinated in Siva's special recipe — barbecued on skewers in the "Tandoor"

**SNOCKEY'S**
Seafood                                                    $

Snockey's has the distinction of being the only restaurant
where a waitress argued me out of the amount of food I
wanted. "You have that (the box oyster stew) and you
don't want nothing else," she warned. She was, of course,
right. Snockey's will soon be 70-years old and salty service
is part of the style of this traditional Philadelphian oyster
house. Four years ago, the restaurant was forced by urban
renewal to move from its marvelous, high-ceilinged, deliciously decaying old location on South Eighth Street to a
new space in Queen Village. In the new spot the plants and
the gaudy fish trophy overhead may be fake but the food is
genuinely fresh. The box stew, incidentally, holds a half-
dozen or so oysters the size of double tablespoons. Fried
clams are so sizzling hot you are warned to eat with care.
Pepper hash is crisp and clear-flavored and the horseradish
you spread on fat oyster crackers will take your breath
away. Based on recent dining experiences, I'd say stick to
staples like hard-shells, stews, freshly opened oysters and
clams and steamed clams—leave the fried and fancy dishes
for the tourists.

SNOCKEY'S OYSTER HOUSE, 1020 South Second Street,
Philadelphia. Telephone: (215) 339-9578. Hours: Monday-
Saturday 11:45 am-11 pm; Sunday 3-10 pm. No cards. No
reservations. Full bar service. Ample street parking.

## SPECIAL SEA FOOD PLATTERS

Whole Broiled Lobster, 1 Deviled Clam, 2 Fried Oysters, Hot Butter Sauce, Cole Slaw **11.00**

**S. AFRICAN ROCK LOBSTER TAIL PLATTER**
1½ Lobster Tail Broiled, Drawn Butter Sauce, F. F. Pot., Cole Slaw **10.00**

Deviled Crab, Shrimp Salad, French Fried Potatoes, Cole Slaw **7.00**

1 Soft Shell Crab, 1 Deviled Clam, ½ Broiled Lobster, Hot Butter Sauce, French Fried Potatoes, Cole Slaw. **9.00**

### LOBSTER SALAD PLATTER
Lobster Salad, French Fr. Potatoes, Cole Slaw **7.00**

### DEVILED CLAM PLATTER
2 Deviled Clams, French Fried Potatoes, Cole Slaw. **3.75**

### COMBINATION PLATTER
Fried Scallops, 1 Deviled Clam, 2 Fried Oysters or Clams, Tartar Sauce, French Fried Potatoes, Cole Slaw **5.60**

### SOFT SHELL CRAB PLATTER
2 Soft Shell Crabs, Tartar Sauce, French Fried Potatoes, Sliced Tomatoes **7.50**

### SPECIAL SEA FOOD PLATTER
Fried Scallops, French Fried Potatoes, Cole Slaw, Tartar Sauce, **4.00**

Stuffed Tomato with Crab Meat or Shrimp Salad, French Fried Potatoes, Cole Slaw **5.75**

| | |
|---|---|
| ½ Cold Lobster, Crab Meat Cocktail and Shrimp ................... (Lobster Broiled 25c extra) | **9.00** |
| Imperial Crab Platter, French Fried Potatoes, Cole Slaw ............ | **6.75** |
| 3 Fried Oysters, Crab Meat Cocktail and Shrimp .................... | **6.25** |
| Clams Casino, Deviled Crab, French Fr. Pot., Cole Slaw, Sl. Tom. .... | **6.25** |
| Fried Shrimp, Tartar Sauce, French Fr. Pot., Cole Slaw ...... | **5.75** |
| Special Deviled Crab, Cole Slaw, French Fried Potatoes .......... | **5.00** |
| 3 Fried Oysters or Clams, Crab Salad or Shrimp Salad and Fr. Fries ....... | **6.25** |
| Barbecued Oysters ½ Doz. .......ala Carte ....... | **3.90** |
| Hot Shrimps with Butter Sauce, ala Carte .............. | **3.00** |

# STROLLI RESTAURANT
Italian            $

Look for Strolli's under "restaurants" in the Yellow Pages and you won't find it. It's listed under "taverns." A clerical error put the tiny South Philadelphia trattoria in the wrong category years ago and John Strolli says it wasn't worth the trouble of trying to change it. Reached by phone the morning after a meal at his "tavern," Strolli laughed as he explained the mix up. Despite the obstacles to locating Strolli's, it's a rare night when the restaurant isn't bustling. (Reservations are a good idea most nights and a must on weekends.) Strolli feels that the attraction isn't the setting. "I put my money in the food," he says. After our food-knowledgeable friend and I were inclined to agree. Our tabletop wasn't much bigger than a large cafeteria tray and it was tucked into a snug space between the dining room and the bar. A paper placemat served as our menu. Fifty cents brought a cup of remarkable escarole soup. For $2.25 we had large portions of fettuccine Alfredo with long, refreshingly chewy ribbons of pasta in a silky sauce of cream, butter and cheese. With the pasta there was veal piccanti, a small serving of lemon and herb-sauced veal that was as flavorful as that encountered elsewhere at twice the $2.60 price tag. My partner's stuffed eggplant was pleasingly priced at $2.25. Our desserts were from a local bakery and unexceptional. We drank coffee and between us a total of three cocktails. The bill? Less than $20. Other bargains from Carmela Strolli's kitchen include spaghetti with fresh clam sauce at $2.25, pasta and beans at $1.45, homemade gnocchi or ravioli at $1.75 and a crabcake platter at the same price. If you're feeling really extravagant, you can order filet mignon with salad and spaghetti for $6. Strolli says he loses money on some items like the jumbo shrimp cocktail ($4.25), but because of volume and low overhead, he comes out alright in the long run. Besides, says Strolli, Carmela *likes* to cook.

STROLLI RESTAURANT, 1528 Dickinson Street, Philadelphia. Telephone: (215) 336-3390. Lunch: 11:30 am-1
pm. Dinner: from 5:30 pm; closed Sunday. No cards.
Reservations accepted. Full bar service. Street parking.

# Italian Dinners

| | |
|---|---|
| SPAGHETTI with SHRIMP | 2.50 |
| SPAGHETTI, MARINARA SAUCE | 1.70 |
| SPAGHETTI, MEAT BALLS OR SAUSAGE | 1.85 |
| SPAGHETTI, OIL & GARLIC | 1.60 |
| SPAGHETTI with FRESH CLAM SAUCE | 2.25 |
| ALFREDO-FETTUCINI | 2.25 |
| RIGATONI | 1.60 |
| with MEAT BALLS or SAUSAGE | 1.95 |
| PASTA & BEANS | 1.45 |
| PASTA & CECI | 1.45 |
| HOMEMADE RAVIOLI | 1.75 |
| with MEAT BALLS or SAUSAGE | 2.50 |
| HOMEMADE GNOCCHI | 1.75 |
| with MEAT BALLS or SAUSAGE | 2.50 |
| VEAL PICCANTI | 2.60 |
| with SPAGHETTI | 3.30 |
| with RAVIOLI or GNOCCHI | 3.40 |
| VEAL SCALLOPINE | 3.25 |
| with SPAGHETTI | 3.60 |
| with RAVIOLI or GNOCCHI | 3.70 |
| VEAL CUTLET PARMAGIAN | 3.25 |
| with SPAGHETTI | 3.60 |
| with RAVIOLI or GNOCCHI | 3.70 |
| STUFFED EGGPLANT PARMAGIAN | 2.25 |
| with SPAGHETTI | 2.85 |
| with RAVIOLI or GNOCCHI | 2.95 |
| STUFFED SHELLS | 2.75 |
| ESCAROLE with OIL & GARLIC | 1.25 |

## Philadelphia: Chestnut Hill (Northwest)
## TELL ERHARDT'S
## CHESTNUT HILL HOTEL
International                                         $$

On TV, German-born Chef Tell Erhardt is the tall, ruggedly handsome man who shares, in a few minutes each evening, chef's secrets from years of European training. In his cooking school, Erhardt teaches more serious students the essentials of haute cuisine. But suppose you'd rather eat than learn to duplicate the chef's dishes? Then there's Chef Tell's Chestnut Hill Hotel, a sophisticated dining room with European manners and menu. The hotel tempts with a more than routinely interesting array of appetizers including Swedish gravlax, homemade and served with an excellent herb-mustard sauce, and steak tartar (the latter also available as an entrée). On one early menu, a special treat was Lady Curzon soup, an incredible creation of turtle essence, laced with wine, floated with heavy cream and so rich that a demitasse serving satisfied. Chef Tell's entrées run to substantial amounts of beef, veal, pork or lamb, served with classic sauces like Périgord, Béarnaise, Choron. There are always some extravagant pastry desserts, but my favorite sweet here is an embarassment of riches called coupe Xeres, a combination of pear sherbet, poached pear, caramel sauce and pear brandy.

TELL ERHARDT'S CHESTNUT HILL HOTEL, 8229 Germantown Avenue, Philadelphia. Telephone: (215) 247-2100. Dinner: Wednesday-Saturday 6-10; Sunday 5-9. Closed Monday and Tuesday. Cards: AE, DC, MC, VISA. Reservations advised. Full bar service. Free parking.

## APPETIZERS

PATÉ MAISON with *Sauce Cumberland*     $2.80

RAGOUT FIN with *Princess Sauce*     3.00

RUSSIAN EGGS with *Caviar*     3.50

ESCARGOT 'ALSACIENNE'     4.50

SWEDISH GRAVLAX     4.80
*(homemade with mustard-herb sauce)*

POACHED FILET of SOLE 'DUGLERE'     5.50
*with Salmon Mousse and Sauce Velouté*

BEEFSTEAK TARTAR made *tableside for two*     8.50
*(Also served as entrée for one)*

## ENTREES

SAUTEED PORK LOIN 'HUNGARIAN STYLE'     $7.80
*in a delicious Paprike Sauce with Spaetzle*

NOISETTE of LAMB 'GASCONE'     8.80
*with vegetable du jour*

BROILED BROCHETTE 'RHODOS'     9.20
*with rice pilaw in a mild curry sauce*

SCHWEINEPFEFFER *(thin pork strips sauteed*     10.50
*with fresh mushrooms, served over spaetzle)*

SAUTEED CHICKEN BREAST 'SUPREME'     10.50
*with fresh asparagus, Sauce Mousseline and rice*

'MATELOTE' *(Filet of Sole, Quenelles, Shrimp,*     12.50
*Sauce Badenia, Rice)*

DOVER SOLE 'BELLE MEUNIERE'     13.00
*sauteed in butter with lemon juice and herbs*

PRIME NEW YORK STEAK 'MAITRE d'HOTEL'     13.00
*with vegetable du jour*

ROASTED DUCK (½) 'MY WAY'     13.50
*with red cabbage and potato puffs*

VEAL STEAK 'GODARD' with *Morilles*     13.50
*in Sauce Perigord*

VEAL MEDALLION 'DIPLOMATE'     14.00
*with Rice Derby and asparagus*

TOURNEDOS 'HENRY IV' *with artichoke bottom,*     14.50
*Sauce Bernaise, Pommes Dauphin*

ENTRECOTE DOUBLE, JARDINIERE des LEGUMES     30.00
*(double sirloin of steak with bouquetiere of*
*vegetables, Sauce Choron) - for two -*

## Philadelphia: Center City
## THAI ROYAL BARGE
Thai $$

The ghost of an early tenant, a formica-and-chrome sand-
wich shop, haunts this place despite some gaudy efforts at
exorcism via imported Thai bric-a-brac. There's been talk
over the years of moving to a classier setting but loyal fans
pooh-pooh the notion, preferring the present location
which tends to discourage less-than-serious Thaiophiles. The
cuisine is exotic but don't fret if you're unfamiliar with the
terrain. Inside the menu there's a page, complete with map,
telling you what cooks in Thai kitchens, and if you forgot
your specs, friendly advice will be forthcoming at the drop
of a knife. That's an inside joke, folks, because Thai food is
pre-cut into spoon-and-fork manageable pieces, hence
knives are not included in place settings. For a clue to the
food, I'd say to expect garlic, hot pepper and some unfamil-
iar flavors like lemony lemon grass and a leaf that looks like
bay but is actually wild lime. If you'd like a personal
recommendation, I'd say try the ob moh din, a casserole
crammed with spicy, in-shell shrimp. It's the menu's priciest
offering but the amount of shrimp easily justifies the cost.
For fun, there are appetizers described on the menu as
deep-fried "surprised" balls with spicy sauce. I'll tell you
that they're chewy meatballs, but don't tell them. It might
spoil the surprise.

THE THAI ROYAL BARGE, 23rd and Sansom Streets,
Philadelphia. Telephone: (215) 567-2542. Hours: daily
4:30 pm-10 pm. Cards: AE, DC, MC, VISA. Reservations
advised. No bar; bring your own wine. Street parking.

## Specialties of the House

- •THAI DELIGHT•A combination of pork, beef and chicken with
  vegetables and sauce.................................$5.95

- •OB MOH DIN•Shellfish baked in an earthen pot with spices
  Shrimps in the shell................................. 11.95
  Clams................................................ 6.95

- •PLA TOD GROB•Crispy fried fish topped with spicy sweet and
  sour sauce......................Priced according to size

- •PET OB NUM PAUNG•Honey-glazed roasted duck half with rice,
  vegetables and gravy.................................9.95

## Thai Curry
(Cooked in coconut cream and served with rice and cucumber salad)

- •GANG MUSMUN NUA•Beef and peanuts in a sweet and sour brown
  curry................................................ 5.95

- •GANG PED PET YANG•Sliced roast duck in a hot curry with
  tomatoes............................................. 6.50

- •GANG PA•Hot curry soup with bamboo shoots and
  beef................................................. 5.95
  chicken..............................................6.25

## Hot and Spicy Food
(The intensity of the spiciness can be altered to suit your taste.)

- •PUD PED• Spicy curry sauté with bamboo shoots and
  beef................................................. 5.95
  chicken.............................................. 6.25
  jumbo shrimp......................................... 6.95

- •PUD PRIG•A sauté of garlic and pepper sauce with bamboo
  shoots and
  beef................................................. 4.75
  chicken.............................................. 5.00
  jumbo shrimp......................................... 5.75
  squid................................................ 4.95

- •NUA SUP GAREE•Sautéed minced beef in curry sauce on a bed
  of rice noodles...................................... 4.50

- •KAO PUD PRIG•Spicy fried rice with bamboo shoots, peppers,&
  pork................................................. 4.50
  beef................................................. 4.75
  jumbo shrimp......................................... 5.75

## Mild but Tasty Food

- •PLA JIEN•Steamed fish with pork, ginger and bean sauce
  Flounder or pompano...............Priced according to size

- •NUA PU PUD HED•Crab meat with straw mushrooms in
  lobster sauce
  Queen crab meat...................................... 7.95
  King crab meat.......................................10.95

- •GOONG PUD PUG GARD KAO•Stir-fried cabbage or bean sprouts
  with jumbo shrimp.................................... 4.75

- •GOONG LOBSTER SAUCE•Jumbo shrimp in lobster sauce.......... 5.25

- •PUD PLIEW WAN GOONG•Sweet and sour shrimp with cucumber,
  tomatoes and onions.................................. 5.25

- •KAO NHA GAI•Sautéed chicken with straw mushrooms and bamboo
  shoots on a bed of rice.............................. 4.75

## Philadelphia: Center City
## 20TH STREET CAFÉ
International $$

The 20th Street Café is in the same high-rent neighborhood where chef Lewis Bolno first made his reputation as a culinary boy wonder in another similarly trendy spot a half-dozen years ago. Bolno knows the folks he feeds well enough to realize that to keep them interested and coming back for more he has to dish up the current "in" combinations. At the moment these include pasta primavera and aioli (served with poached cod and vegetables), as well as a campy chili named for Liz Taylor. The restaurant opened sans liquor license and with food prices that were fairly lean. Although the former changed, it remains one of this town's more reasonable places to take a date (of the same or opposite sex) or to dine alone on the way home from the office. Expect the setting to be fashionably bright and stark, however.

20TH STREET CAFÉ, 261 South 20th Street, Philadelphia. Telephone: (215) 546-6867. Lunch: Monday-Saturday from 11:30. Dinner: Monday-Saturday 6-11. Sunday brunch 11-3. Cards: AE, MC, VISA. Reservations advised. Full bar service. Street parking.

**Pasta Primavera**     5.50
pasta tossed with fresh vegetables,
heavy cream and parmesan cheese

**Chili Elizabeth Taylor**     5.00
a spicy chili topped with cornbread,
and served with black beans and a vegetable chutney

**Aïoli**     5.50
chilled poached cod served with assorted vegetables
and a garlic mayonnaise

**Filet of Flounder**     6.75
poached in vermouth with cucumbers, served
with crème fraîche and red caviar

**Fried Chicken**     6.75

**Pork Chops Forestière**     7.75
a sautéed porkchop with a red sauce with
bacon, shallots, mushrooms, and new potatoes

**Veal Scallops**     9.75
sautéed with tomatoes and artichoke hearts in
lemon juice and vermouth

**Veal Kidneys**     7.75
sautéed, served in a madiera and
dijon mustard sauce

**Nymphs aux champagne**     9.50
frogs legs sautéed, with a sauce of
champagne, shallots, and heavy cream

**Canard aux Cassis**     10.00
duck served with a black currant
liquor sauce

**Steak Flambé**     11.00
sautéed strip steak with a butter and
gin flambé

# Philadelphia: Chestnut Hill (Northwest)
# UNDER THE BLUE MOON
## International                    $$

Under the Blue Moon seats about 30 in each of its two small dining rooms and it puts folks in such close proximity that dining here for the first time seems a little like signing up for a vacation at a nudist camp. You'll be fine, though, if you know in advance what to expect. Something about the chemistry of the place breaks down aloofness and owner Gene Gosfield says he's seen more than one friendship formed over adjoining dinner tables. The restaurant offers what Gosfield and his wife (who does the cooking) call "New York Times cooking carried to a professional level." Seen fit to print on a recent menu were a Spanish seafood dish, Chinese walnut duck, sesame pecan chicken, Congolese steak and veal with fragrant mushroom sauce. Specials of the day are written on table tents. Also on the tents are the desserts of the day, delectables like Texas chocolate or Curaçao banana cakes, coffee buttercrunch pie and chilled lemon soufflé with raspberry sauce. Blue Moon recently gained a liquor license and Gosfield says he's working hard to keep the wine selection interesting yet affordable.

UNDER THE BLUE MOON, 8042 Germantown Avenue, Philadelphia. Telephone: (215) 247-1100. Hours: Tuesday-Thursday 6 pm-8:45 pm; Friday to 9:45 pm; Saturday to 10:45. No cards. Reservations recommended on weekends. Full bar service. Street parking.

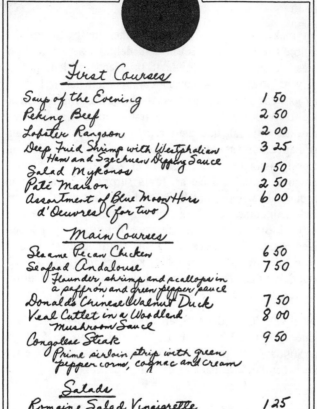

## First Courses

| | |
|---|---|
| Soup of the Evening | 1 50 |
| Peking Beef | 2 50 |
| Lobster Rangoon | 2 00 |
| Deep Fried Shrimp with Westphalian Ham and Szechuen Dipping Sauce | 3 25 |
| Salad Mykonos | 1 50 |
| Paté Maison | 2 50 |
| Assortment of Blue Moon Hors d'Oeuvres (for two) | 6 00 |

## Main Courses

| | |
|---|---|
| Sesame Pecan Chicken | 6 50 |
| Seafood Andalouse | 7 50 |
| Flounder, shrimp and scallops in a saffron and green pepper sauce | |
| Donald's Chinese Walnut Duck | 7 50 |
| Veal Cutlet in a Woodland Mushroom Sauce | 8 00 |
| Congolese Steak | 9 50 |
| Prime sirloin strip with green peppercorns, cognac and cream | |

## Salads

| | |
|---|---|
| Romaine Salad Vinaigrette | 1 25 |
| Manderin Salad | 2 25 |
| Spinach, orange, chicken and toasted almonds in a sesame dressing | |
| Coffee and Various Teas | 50 |

## under the blue moon

## VINCENZO'S
Italian                                            $$

What makes this restaurant worth mentioning is not the
location (in rowhouse South Philadelphia where parking
spaces are inherited). Nor is it the decor which, put as
kindly as possible, resembles a combination bar and meet-
ing room for a slightly down-at-the-heels fraternal organiza-
tion. It's Vincenzo's very good Italian food. Some of the
dishes are unusual, like the crespelle Belvedere, the restau-
rant's appetizing stack of thin, delicate crêpes filled with an
antipasto assortment of meats, tuna, vegetables and topped
with sour cream and caviar. It's a surprising combination
but one that works beautifully. Other dishes worth recom-
mending include the thick, mushroom soup and the spa-
ghetti di Bruno, with its creamy, slightly sharp pepper-
spiked sauce. For dessert try the crumb-crusted ricotta
cheese pie or the homemade ice cream flavored with
almond liqueur. The restaurant has a selection of Califor-
nian, Italian and French wines.

VINCENZO'S, 1208 Tasker Street, Philadelphia. Tele-
phone: (215) 339-9325. Hours: Tuesday-Saturday 5:30-10
pm; Sunday 4-10 pm. Closed Monday. Cards: AE. Reserva-
tions accepted. Full bar service. Street parking.

The Columbia Club

## Philadelphia: Center City
## THE WAY WE WERE
Continental

**$$**

There are just eight tables at the Way We Were and they are near enough to one another to make loving your neighbor fairly important to the enjoyment of a meal here. The Lombard Street storefront is highly personal, cozy, decorated with an interesting collection of antiques and collectibles (all for sale). Two booths are curtained like gothic four-poster beds. The menu is appropriately small but with a nice balance of choices. There are interesting, sausage-stuffed appetizers and good country pâté on the appetizer list. Entrées usually include something beefy, like steak au poivre, something elegant but inexpensive like chicken, something sophisticated like veal and a fresh fish catch of the day. The restaurant serves a popular Sunday brunch that features a variety of egg dishes and crêpes with crabmeat and avocado. There's no liquor license but you're warned of that when you make your reservations. Wine brought from home will be uncorked expertly and your glasses kept filled.

THE WAY WE WERE, 20th and Lombard Streets, Philadelphia. Telephone: (215) 735-2450. Hours: Tuesday-Sunday 6 pm-10 pm. Sunday brunch 11:30-3. Cards: DC, MC, VISA. Reservations advised. No alcoholic beverages; bring your own wine. Street parking.

## Appetizers

| | |
|---|---|
| Avacado Louis XIV | 2.95 |
| Country Pate' | 3.25 |
| Crepes | 3.25 |
| Stuffed Mushrooms | 3.00 |
| Sauteed Chicken Livers | 2.75 |
| Crabmeat Remick | 3.75 |
| | |
| Soup du Jour | 2.00 |
| Salade | 1.75 |

## — Entrees —

| | |
|---|---|
| Roast Duckling | 8.50 |
| Veal Oscar | 8.95 |
| Veal Lafayette | 8.95 |
| Calfs Liver | 7.50 |
| Steak au Poivre | 10.50 |
| Catch of the Day | ~ |
| Poulet Rochambeau | 7.50 |

## Philadelphia: East Philly
## WILDFLOWERS
### International

**$$**

The wildflowers in the name are depicted on a full wall of glorious, stained-glass panels that, like every other reflecting surface in this immaculately maintained restaurant, sparkle with care. Wildflowers first gained local attention for a salad buffet that offered more, better and fresher choices than any other in town. Lately the restaurant has been making friends with its policy of offering wines at prices just a notch above retail. For those who insist on more than a salad and wine, there's the long menu, one that doesn't miss a single stop on the culinary map. Represented are the Caribbean (fruit soup), the Middle East (shashlik), the Mediterranean ("scampi"), Germany (oysters Bremerhafen) and, of course, France (everything from liver pâté in puff pastry to chocolate mousse.) There's a tempting selection of desserts, but if nothing seems just right for your sweet tooth, consider something from the full page of exotic coffees. Or a drink from the bar's extensive selection of Cognac, cordials, liqueurs and vintage fortified wines.

WILDFLOWERS, 514 South Fifth Street, Philadelphia. Telephone: (215) 923-6708. Hours: Monday 5:30 pm-10 pm; Tuesday-Thursday to 11 pm; Friday and Saturday to midnight; Sunday brunch 11-3, dinner from 4:30. Cards: AE, MC, VISA. Reservations advised. Full bar service. Street parking.

## POISSON

**ESCALOPE DE SAUMON POCHÉ BELLE VUE, FROID** 8.95
*Cold poached salmon with cucumber dill sauce.*

**ESCALOPE DE SAUMON GRILLÉ MAITRE D'HOTEL** 8.95
*Northwestern salmon filet broiled with fresh herb butter.*

**SCAMPI GAMBERETTI ALLA MARINA** 8.50
*Shrimp, garlic and herbs sauteed in white wine and butter.*

**COQUILLES DE ST. JACQUES À LA PARISIENNE** 6.95
*Scallops and fresh mushrooms in wine and cream sauce, au gratin.*

**FILLET OF BLUEFISH TAMARI** 5.95
*Broiled fresh bluefish with white wine and a virgin soy sauce.*

**TRUITE SAUTÉ BELLE MEUNIERE AMANDINE** 6.95
*Fresh water trout pan fried in butter with almonds.*

**FILET DE SOLE MEUNIERE À LA PROVENCALE** 6.50
*Filet of sole dipped in egg, sauteed in butter with mushrooms, white wine and herbs.*

 ## VIANDE ET VOLAILLE

**VITELLO SAUTE MILANAISE CON PASTA** 8.25
*Veal tender saute with Pruscutto ham, mushroom duxelle, tomato sauce, served with pasta.*

**VEAL OSCAR BIEN GARNI** 9.95
*Veal tender sauteed with Alaskan king crabmeat, asparagus spears and Bearnaise sauce.*

**WIENER SCHNITZEL AVEC POMMES DU TERRE LYONNAISE** 7.25
*Breaded veal tender, pan fried in lemon butter and served with Lyonnaise potatoes.*

**RIS DE VEAU PERIGOURDINE** 7.75
*Calves sweetbreads and fresh mushrooms in a truffled sauce demi-glace, flambed with cognac and madeira.*

**BREAST OF CURRIED CHICKEN DJAKARTA** 5.95
*Boneless breast of chicken sauteed with coconut milk, oriental mellon and crisp vegetables, served with rice.*

**BREAST OF CHICKEN DOMINIQUE** 5.95
*Boneless breast of chicken sauteed with artichoke hearts, asparagus, mushrooms and cognac in sauce demi-glace.*

 ## ROTIS

**FILET MIGNON GRILLÉ À LA BÉARNAISE** 9.25
*Charcoal broiled tenderloin steak with Bearnaise sauce and French fried potatoes.*

**ENTRECOTE GRILLE À LA BÉARNAISE** 10.95
*Prime cut sirloin strip steak, charcoal broiled and served with French fried potatoes and Bearnaise sauce.*

**LE DEMI CARRE D'AGNEAU À LA FRANCAISE** 12.75
*Rack of lamb roasted with Dusseldorf mustard and garlic herbed bread crumbs.*

**CANARD ROTI POIVRADE** 8.95
*Boneless roast duckling flambed in Madagascar green peppercorn sauce.*

## THE GRAND SALAD BUFFET

**SALAD BUFFET WITH ENTREE** 1.95

**SALAD BUFFET A LA CARTE** 4.95

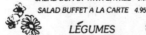

## LÉGUMES

**ASPARAGUS AU BEIRRE or SAUCE HOLLANDAISE** 1.75

**SAUTEED FRESH SPINACH IN HERB BUTTER** 1.50

**SLICED MUSHROOMS SAUTEED IN BROWN BUTTER** 1.75

**STIR FRIED SNOW PEAS** 2.00

**FRENCH FRIED ONION RINGS** 1.50

**PARSLEY POTATOES** 1.25

**FRENCH FRIED POTATOES** 1.25

**LYONNAISE POTATOES** 1.50

# Berks County

**BLAIR CREEK INN**
International                                               **$$**

Unless you live nearer to Allentown than Philadelphia, give
yourself plenty of time to get to this newly revived country
inn. Better yet, make a visit to Blair Creek Inn part of a day
of sightseeing in the pretty local countryside. The Blair of
the inn's name is an attractive, attentive, gray-haired man
who gives his guests the feeling he's genuinely pleased to
have them at his table. Dinner begins with a small crock of
creamy cheese spread accompanied with cellophane-
wrapped crackers and bread sticks to nibble while you
study the menu. Good first courses include steak tartar—
fresh, lean ground beef with egg yolk, chopped onion and
capers for your own mixing. The inn buys prime, aged beef

Blair Creek Inn
Fine Country Cooking

Mertztown, Pennsylvania 19539    215 682-6700
                                 215 682-4300         Innkeeper, Blair

for its charcoal-broiled steaks but if you'd rather test the kitchen than the butcher, order one of the house specialties like veal piccata, sliced paper thin, sautéed and finally sauced with lemon-spiked wine, or the excellent, trim and tiny frogs legs. A variety of fresh vegetables, crisp-cooked and buttery, is served family style The bread basket usually boasts crusty rolls, French bread and something sweet, warm and wonderful like homemade zucchini bread. Desserts are baked here also. The pecan pie is generous with the pecans and topped with real whipped cream. There's no wine list. Instead, a basket filled with the available bottles comes to your table on the arm of your waiter or waitress. As might be imagined, that limits the choices to a totable number. The inn's Sunday brunch invites you to relax and enjoy the day's newspapers as you eat your way through a prix fixe feast that begins with juice and coffee, followed by pastries and a main course of quiche, eggs, chicken and waffles, steak or the inn's exceptional French toast made from yeast baba dipped in heavy cream and beaten egg.

BLAIR CREEK INN, Mertztown, Pennsylvania (between Allentown and Reading). Telephone: (215) 682-6700. Hours: dinner, Tuesday-Saturday 5:30 pm-10 pm; Sunday brunch 11 am-2:30 pm. Cards: AE, VISA. Reservations essential on weekends. Telephone ahead for directions. Full bar service. Free parking.

# Fare of The Dinner

**Steak Tartar** 3¹⁵  **Escargots**    **Appetizers**

**Jumbo Shrimp Cocktail** 3⁹³  **King Crabmeat Cocktail**

**Sour Cream Quiche Lorraine** 2⁸⁵

**Blair Creek French Onion Soup** 2⁴⁵    **Soups**

**Cuban Black Bean Soup** served with accompaniments 2⁵⁰

**Innkeeper's Choice of Soup** 1⁵²

**Fresh Spinach Salad**    **Salads**
Hot Bacon Dressing, Mushrooms, Sliced Eggs and Bacon 1⁷⁵

**Blair Creek Tossed Salad** 1⁵⁵  **Sliced Tomatoes** 1²⁵

## Please Ask to See Our Wine Baskets
## & Features of the Day

**Charcoal Broiled New York Sirloin Strip Steak** Ask waiter  **Entrees**

**Charcoal Broiled Filet Mignon** 11⁵⁰

**Specialties of**
**The Inn**

**Steak & Quail**
Filet with Quail served with Hunter Sauce and Rice 11⁹⁵

**Blair Creek Chicken Curry**
Boned Breast of Chicken with Chutney and Complements 9⁵⁰

**Veal Piccata**
Served with a Light Wine Sauce and a Touch of Lemon 10⁹⁵

**Chef David's Baby Frog Legs**
Sauteed in Fresh Herb Butter 11⁹⁵

**King Crab**
Sauteed in Orange Butter Sauce 9⁹⁵

**Scallops Jean**
Scallops Broiled in Butter with Bacon and Hazelnuts 8⁶⁵

**Scampi Diane**
Scallops and Shrimp in a Garlic, Herb Butter Sauce 9⁹⁵

**Irish Coffee**    **Three Vegetables**    **Desserts**
a la carte   Served with Entree   Creations of the Chef
a la carte

## Please Spend the Better Part of an Evening With Us

139

## Berks County: Reading
## GREEN HILLS INN
French                                                $$$

The Green Hills is almost too good to be true. It is old (the original tavern dates to 1805) and correspondingly quaint. There are bright bouquets of fresh flowers on each of the dining room tables and a real fireplace with great, fat logs lines the length of the long porch, in anticipation of chilly nights to come. The young owner-chef is so dedicated that to broaden his horizons he apprenticed himself to Philadelphia's most celebrated French chef, Georges Perrier. For several years, in addition to overseeing the kitchen at his inn, he made weekly trips to Philadelphia to work from noon until midnight with Perrier. Such effort would be wasted, of course, without talent, but that is here too, which may be the reason why despite an out-of-the-way location the restaurant prospers. The Green Hills menu has gone gradually from a mixture of French and American dishes to a full French list that reflects the growing sophistication of local diners. Pressed for recommendations, I'd have to suggest the delicate quenelles or the boneless squab with its delicious forcemeat stuffing. Almost any dessert is certain to please, but I particularly like the frozen Grand Marnier soufflé influenced by Perrier's version at Le Bec Fin. In addition to the regular menu, Green Hills has daily specials dictated by the treasures found in the market that day. Fresh raspberries and perfect peaches from local growers may inspire the chef to add a superlative peche Melba to the dessert list, or fresh salmon might inspire saumon au beurre blanc.

GREEN HILLS INN, Route 10, Reading, Pennsylvania. (10 miles north of the Pennsylvania Turnpike Morgantown exit). Telephone: (215) 777-9611. Lunch: Tuesday-Friday 11:30-1:30. Dinner: Tuesday-Friday 5:30-9; Saturday 5:30-9:30. Closed Sunday and Monday. No cards; personal checks accepted. Reservations advised. Full bar service. Free parking.

140

# Green Hills Inn — SINCE 1805

## Les Hors d'oeuvres

| | | | |
|---|---|---|---|
| Quennelles De Brochet-Sauce Americaine | three fifty | Coquilles St. Jacques À La Bretonne | three fifty |
| Cervelas De Fruits De Mer | three fifty | Pate Maison En Croute | two fifty |
| Escargots Chablisienne | three fifty | Terrine De Turbot | ten fifty |
| Saumon Fumé D'Ecosse — Smoked Scotch Salmon | four fifty | Les Potages Du Jour | |

## Les Entrees

| | |
|---|---|
| Feuillete De Truite – d'Estragon – Brook Trout in Puff Pastry | nine fifty |
| Filet De Boeuf Chambertin – Filet Mignon with Red Wine Sauce | ten fifty |
| Crabe Bernadette – Backfin Crabmeat Baked with Mushrooms and wine | nine fifty |
| Chateaubriand Berrichone – Double Filet Mignon with Bordelaise Sauce Served with an array of Fresh Vegetables (FOR 2) | twenty four |
| Escalopes De Veau Chasseur – Tender Milk Fed Veal with a Classic Mushroom and Tomato Sauce | nine fifty |
| Carre D'Agneau Au Jus – Roast Rack of Spring Lamb served with Natural juices | twelve fifty |
| Mousse De Homard Beurre Blanc – Lobster and Salmon with Butter Sauce | ten fifty |
| Filet De Boeuf Ammarie – Thick Slices Filet Mignon, Delicately Sauted, served with a Truffle Sauce | nine ninety five |
| Foie De Veau Bercy – Baby Calf's Liver Sauted with Shallots, Chablis and Veal Stock | eight ninety five |
| Homard Thermidor – Fresh Maine Lobster (when available) | sixteen |
| Supreme De Volaille Aux Chanterelles – Breast of Chicken Sauted with Wild Mushrooms | nine fifty |
| Steak Au Poivre Vert – Sirloin Steak Seasoned with Green Peppercorn Sauce | ten fifty |
| La Sole Grenobloise – Sole Sauted with Lemon and Capers | eight ninety five |
| Escalopes De Veau Normande – Veal Scallops with Cream, Mushrooms and Calvados | nine fifty |

## Les Desserts

| | | | |
|---|---|---|---|
| Glaces Et Sorbets | one twenty five | Mousse Au Chocolat | one fifty |
| Fraises Romanoff — Strawberries with whipped cream and wine | one ninety five | Les Patisseries De La Maison | one ninety five |
| Cheese Cake | one ninety five | Cafe | fifty |
| Souffle Glace Grand Marnier | | The | fifty |
| À La Green Hills | one ninety five | Espresso | seventy five |

All Above Entrees Include
Legumes Du Jour

## Berks County: Oley
## THE INN AT OLEY
French

$$

It doesn't take long to realize that what looks at first glance like a typical sleepy Pennsylvania farm-town hotel is something quite different. Step across the broad porch of Oley's inn, open the door and sniff. Close your eyes and you're transported to one of the famous food towns of central France. Let the seductive aroma lead you past the bar, with its old-fashioned wood stove and tin ceiling, into dining rooms where the linens are crease free, the flowers vividly fresh and the cuisine imaginative. The classics are here as well as examples of nouvelle cuisine dishes. Among the latter are red snapper marinated in coriander and lime, baked and then served with lobster sauce, and navarin of sea scallops glossed with a creamy white wine sauce and accompanied with color-bright, flavorful vegetables. Chef Jean-Maurice Juge trained in Lyons, France, the birthplace of nouvelle cuisine. He incorporates the new feel for French food in daily specialties like sea bass cooked in seaweed, gigot of spring chicken with garden greens, veal with cream, basil and avocado. The wine selection does its best to measure up to the food.

THE INN AT OLEY, Main Street, Oley, Pennsylvania. Telephone: (215) 987-3459. Hours: Tuesday-Saturday 5:30 pm-10 pm. Cards: MC, VISA. Reservations advised. Full bar service. Street parking.

## To start

| | |
|---|---|
| Baby lobster tails in a light beer batter | $4.25 |
| Gratin of salmon with sorrel sauce | $3.25 |
| A cold salad of duckling and pheasant, vinaigrette | $4.25 |
| Terrine of crayfish and salmon in a mousse of trout | $3.95 |
| Gateau of sweetbreads in a sauce of fresh thyme | $3.95 |
| Mushrooms stuffed with clams and covered with Bearnaise | $3.25 |
| Escargots Brillat Savarin | $3.95 |

## Soups

| | |
|---|---|
| Mussel soup flavored with saffron and baked under a layer of puff pastry | $3.25 |
| Cream of fresh carrot soup | $1.75 |
| The Inn's Onion Soup | $2.25 |

## Entrées

*Served with fresh vegetables in season and a salad presenting the best of today's crop.*

### Le Canard a la Facon du Chef $ 9.25

Young Long Island duckling roasted to perfection, with crisp brown skin, yet moist flesh, then served with Chef Juge's sauce of the day.

### Tournedos Bercy $11.95

Slices of filet, prepared to your order, with a light sauce of shallots, veal stock and white wine.

### Steak au Poivre Parisienne $10.95

Crushed peppercorns are gently pressed into a prime sirloin steak and quickly sauteed by our Chef. The sauce of veal stock, Dijon mustard, shallots and parsley is blended and flamed with Cognac. The steak is also available without peppercorns or sauce.

### Escalope de Veau aux Concombres $ 9.95

Thin slices of sauteed milk fed veal and sliced cucumbers are served with a light sauce of white wine, shallots, tarragon and just a bit of cream.

### Red Snapper au Bouillon de Homard $ 9.95

This popular fresh Florida fish is marinated in coriander and lime, then baked and served with lobster sauce.

### Roast Cornish Game Hen aux Poivre Verts $ 8.95

Spices, including the Inn's own blend of imported green peppercorns, Cognac and pan juices combine to provide a perfect sauce for this young bird.

### Salmis of Pheasant $10.95

A roasted, boneless pheasant, sealed with pastry in an earthenware crock and simmered in its own juices.

### Filet de Boeuf Marchand de Vin $11.95

A thick prime filet prepared to your taste, served with a light Bordelaise sauce, shallots and red wine.

### Navarin of Scallops $ 8.95

Sea scallops poached in white wine and cream and served with an assortment of fresh spring vegetables.

### Lobster Tails du Village Oley $12.95

Young lobster tails are sauteed in lobster butter, flames in Cognac, married to a creamy sauce and returned to bake to a golden brown. We thank Chef Juge for honoring our Village with this original creation.

### Rosemary Roasted Rack of Lamb For One $14.50 — For Two $29.00

The rack of lamb, roasted to order, is delicately seasoned, garnished with fresh vegetables, served with a mild mustard sauce and carved at tableside.

## Berks County: Reading
## JOE'S
### Wild Mushrooms

**$$$**

Wild mushrooms have put this inner-city Reading restaurant on the gastronomic map. Expert mycologists Joe and Wanda Czernicki and fellow mushroom collectors spend months finding palatable, non-toxic specimens that are transformed into an inviting array of appetizers, soups, entrées and side dishes. A meal at Joe's might begin with marinated wild mushrooms (cepes and chanterelles are usually available) that taste mysteriously woodsy and have a wonderfully slippery texture. The mushroom soup is of Czech origin, a brown cream infused with the fragrance and flavor of dried mushrooms. Mushroom piroshki put minced mushrooms in a tender half-moon of sour cream pastry. Several entrées are also mushroom-studded. Desserts aren't, but they're homemade and include Wanda's excellent almond cream cheesecake. There's real espresso to sip afterwards. To find out what lurks in the wine cellar, head for the lobby where bottles are displayed. On our last visit, prices were so high, however, that we beat a hasty retreat. Service at Joe's is genuinely pleasant, but the place has a reputation for whisking you through your meal quickly. If you want to linger, stand your ground.

JOE'S, Seventh and Laurel Streets, Reading, Pennsylvania. Telephone: (215) 373-6794. Hours: Tuesday-Friday 5 pm-9 pm; Saturday 4:30 pm-10 pm. Cards: AE, DC, MC, VISA. Reservations advised. Full bar service. Street parking.

## Berks County: Fleetwood
## MOSELEM SPRINGS INN
### Pennsylvania Dutch/American

$

Far too few country inns feature the food of the rural area in which they are located; Moselem Springs Inn is one that does. A smokehouse out back produces smoky glazed corn beef, sausages and Pennsylvania Dutch meats. The kitchen keeps stride with appropriate additions like an appetizer of pickled tripe, short ribs of beef, stuffed breast of chicken, pan-fried liver with onions. Homey accompaniments include apple fritters, dried corn, Dutch cream slaw, warm spiced applesauce and homebaked bread with thick, dark apple butter. Portions are geared for hearty eaters. Service is designed to make all generations feel welcome. Prices are kept low. Drinks can be fun. Adding to standard bar fare are fruit wines (currant and elderberry), apple daiquiris and whiskey sours served in old-fashioned canning jars. For the young—in age or at heart—the inn provides mugs of real draft birch beer. The inn was built in 1852 to provide food and overnight accommodations for travelers and those hauling goods to and from Philadelphia. Decor is early American, ranging from the formality of the large "Presidential," dining room to the coziness of other, smaller rooms with functioning fireplaces.

MOSELEM SPRINGS INN, US Routes 222 and 662, Fleetwood (between Allentown and Reading), Pennsylvania. Telephone: (215) 944-8213. Hours: Sunday-Thursday 11:30 am-8 pm; closed Friday and Saturday. No cards. Reservations advised. Full bar service. Free parking. Children welcome.

# Bucks County

## Bucks County: Lumberville
## BLACK BASS HOTEL
### American                              $$

It's difficult to imagine a more attractive setting for a meal, whether that meal is brunch, lunch or dinner, than this historic inn on the banks of the Delaware River. In addition to scenic beauty outside and cozy fireplaces and mellow antiques inside, the Black Bass offers friendly service and food that is always interesting, never contrived. Menus, inked on brown wrapping paper, offer early American-sounding choices like Charleston Meeting Street crab, New England lobster pie and Benjamin Franklin's smoked oysters and lamb, as well as more contemporary selections like breast of chicken with hot walnuts and Cornish game hen with wild rice. Desserts include rum cream pie, boysenberry sherbet, deep-dish apple-strawberry pie. A special champagne brunch features juice, eggs Benedict fruit crêpes, sherry creamed beef and cheese or mushroom omelet, coffee or tea at a fixed price of $8.50. The Black Bass is one of the few vintage inns in America that continues to have overnight accommodations. The rooms, furnished handsomely with early American antiques, are a great convenience for the faithful customers who travel great distances to dine here.

BLACK BASS HOTEL, River Road, Lumberville, Pennsylvania. Telephone: (215) 297-5770. Lunch: noon-2. Dinner: 5:30-10. Sunday brunch 1-3. Cards: AE, DC, MC. Reservations suggested. Full bar service. Free parking.

## Bucks County: Doylestown
## CONTI CROSS KEYS INN
### Continental

**$$**

Loyalist friends of King George were the Cross Keys' first patrons; they wouldn't recognize the place today though. Through several expansions, any architectural clues of its early identity have all but vanished. What remains is roomy, comfortable and convenient, sometimes even chic, but never historic. It's doubtful you'll miss the ghosts, however. You'll be too distracted by the pleasures of the table. Since 1945 when the elder Contis purchased the inn, the family has been perfecting both menu and service. A third generation of Contis, grandsons Joseph and Michael, are following in the tradition. The Cross Keys' menu is large, with a full page of seafood entrées and another of poultry and prime meats. Cooking is straightforward with an occasional French or northern Italian flourish (the founding Contis emigrated from Italy's Piedmont region) or an occasional extravagance like lamb Wellington or escargots in puff pastry. The daily lunch is a super bargain for hearty eaters; the specials priced from $5 to $7 offer a variety of entrées along with soup or juice, potato and vegetable, salad, dessert and beverage. Walter Conti, son of the founders, has assembled one of the area's best balanced wine lists and his knowledge of the subject allows for expert guidance in matching a wine with your meal if you desire it

CONTI CROSS KEYS INN, Routes 611 and 313, Doylestown, Pennsylvania. Telephone: (215) 348-3539. Hours: Monday-Friday 11:30 am-11 pm; Saturday 4 pm-11:30 pm; closed Sunday and holidays. Cards: AE, DC, MC, VISA. Reservations advised. Full bar service. Free parking.

LAMB WELLINGTON. . . . . . . . . . . . . . . . . . . . . . . . . . . . . 12.50

INDIVIDUAL RACK OF LAMB (4). . . . . . . . . . . . . . . . . . . 11.50

CALF'S LIVER A LA TURINOISE. . . . . . . . . . . . . . . . . . . . . 9.50
sauteed with onions.

SWEETBREADS "GRENOBLOISE" . . . . . . . . . . . . . . . . 10.00
lemon, butter.

PAILLARD OF VEAL . . . . . . . . . 11.00
a dieter delight · simply broiled veal with lemon.

VEAL SCALLOPINE "ALLA CONTI" . . . . . . . . . . . . . . . . . . . . . 10.00
sauteed in sherry, tomatoes, mushrooms, onions and peppers

VEAL SCALLOPINE "MARSALA" . . . . . . . . . . . . . . . . . . . . . . 10.00
sauteed in marsala wine and mushrooms.

VEAL CUTLET "PARMIGIANA" . . . . . . . . . . . . . . . . . . . . . . 10.00

MILK FED VEAL CUTLET. . . . . . . . . . . . . . . . . . . . . . . . . . . 9.50

BREAST OF CAPON "FORESTIERE" . . . . . . . . . . . . . . . . . . 9.50
white wine, mushrooms, parmesan cheese.

CHICKEN PICCANTE WITH ARTICHOKES. . . . . . . . . . . . . . . . 10.50

MARYLAND LUMP CRABMEAT SAUTEED "NORFOLK". . . . . . . 11.00

LUMP CRABMEAT AU GRATIN . . . . . . . . . . . . . . . . . . . . . 10.50

BROILED CHICKEN LOBSTER WITH CRABMEAT . . . . . . . . . . 13.50

LOBSTER "PROVENCALE" . . . . . . . . . . . . . . . . . . . . . . . . 14.50
sauteed in herb butter with lemon.

MAINE LOBSTER "NEWBURG" . . . . . . . . . . . . . . . . . . . . . . 12.50

JUMBO SOUTH AFRICAN LOBSTER TAIL . . . . . . . . . . . . . . . . 15.00
steamed or broiled.

CONTI'S DEVILED CRABMEAT CUTLET . . . . . . . . . . . . . . . . . . 10.00

WEST INDIAN PRAWNS SAUTE "PROVENCALE" . . . . . . . . . . 11.00

BROILED PRAWNS "SCAMPI ALLA GRIGLIA". . . . . . . . . . . . . 11.00

FRIED JUMBO SHRIMP . . . . . . . . . . . . . . . . . . . . . . . . . . . . 9.50

FRIED SEAFOOD COMBINATION. . . . . . . . . . . . . . . . . . . . . 11.00
deviled crabmeat, shrimp, scallops, frog legs, sole, lobster tail.

COQUILLES ST. JACQUES. . . . . . . . . . . . . . . . . . . . . . . . . . 10.00

SAUTE SCALLOPS "ALLA FRANCAISE" . . . . . . . . . . . . . . . . 10.50

FETTUCINE WITH CRABMEAT. . . . . . . . . . . . . . . . . 9.00

SPAGHETTI ALLA "CARBONARA" . . . . . . . . . . . . . . 8.00
ham, bacon, eggs, peppers, parmesan cheese.

SPAGHETTI ALLA "MARINARA". . . . . . . . . . . . . . . . 6.50
tomatoes, onions, basil, anchovies, fresh garlic.

SPAGHETTI WITH MEAT SAUCE . . . . . . . . . . . . . . . 7.00

SPAGHETTI WITH RED OR WHITE CLAM SAUCE. . . . . 8.00

## Bucks County: Doylestown Area
## GRANDADDYS
## International                                            $$

Grandaddys is a gloriously stylish restaurant quartered in what started life as a sturdy Bucks County barn. Today diners can choose between the windowed front room that probably once housed farm machinery and the twin balconies that were formerly hay lofts. The loft areas provide comfortable seating in booths designed around carved headboards. Dine in bed, or at a conventional table downstairs. Likewise, choose between safe and adventurous dishes. The safe selections include crab quiche that's homemade, with excellent pastry and delicate filling, shrimp cocktail, baked onion soup, prime sirloin, rack of lamb, filet mignon. For the more adventurous there is Chinese Christmas duck, a riot of flavors that might just remind you of an explosion in a Chinese fireworks factory. A charming touch is the sweet butter, molded into the shape of a nesting hen, that arrives with your freshly baked bread. Wines are a pleasant surprise: A good selection is available at reasonable prices.

GRANDADDYS, Route 611 and Almshouse Road, south of Doylestown, Pennsylvania. Telephone: (215) 343-3435. Hours: weekdays 5 pm-11 pm; Friday and Saturday 5 pm-midnight; Sunday 4 pm-9 pm. Cards: AE, DC, MC, VISA. Reservations advised. Full bar service. Free parking.

**CHINESE CHRISTMAS DUCK** ............................. 11.50
*In a Sweet and Sour Sauce, Over Grandaddy's Rice,*
*Flamed Table Side*

**PRIME N. Y. SIRLOIN** ........12.75
*Center Cut Only*
*with Bearnaise Sauce*

**FILET MIGNON** ................ 12.75
*The Finest Served with*
*Bearnaise Sauce*

**PRIME RACK OF LAMB** ....12.75
*A Filet of Spring Lamb*

**VEAL MARCY** ......................10.00
*Saute Veal in a Wine Sauce Topped*
*with Prosciutto Ham and*
*Mozzarella Cheese*

**VEAL LAINEY** ......................11.50
*Saute Veal Topped with Snow Peas*
*Crabmeat and a Special Sauce*

**SOUTH AFRICAN LOBSTER**
**TAIL** ..................................13.50
*Broil Baked To Keep It Juicy*

**COQUILLE SAINT**
**JACQUES** ..........................11.50
*"Our House Specialty" Served in*
*A Puff Pastry Shell*

**PAELLA "Good Friend"** ........12.50
*Lobster, Shrimp, Chicken and*
*Clams Over Saffron Rice*

**FILET OF SOLE** ....................9.50
*Butter Lemon Sauce*

**SOLE OSCAR** ..........................11.00
*Filet of Sole Topped with Asparagus,*
*Crabmeat and Bearnaise Sauce*

**CRABMEAT AU GRATIN** 12.00
*Back Fin Lump Crabmeat*
*in a Cheese Sauce*

**SHRIMP PORTAFINO** ........11.00
*Jumbo Shrimp in a Marinara Sauce*

**SHRIMP SCAMPI** ................10.50
*Shrimp in a Wine and Garlic*
*Butter Sauce*

**LOBSTER SAVANNAH** ............................................................... 12.00
*Vol Au Vent - Under Glass*

## Bucks County: New Hope
## THE HACIENDA
### International                                    $$

Tally up the number of chairs in Pam Minford's Hacienda and you will probably be surprised to realize the place seats well over 100. Dining rooms in this attractively decorated restaurant are small and separate so that even when the house is full you never get the feeling of being lost in a crowd. The central dining room is bowered in dark-background floral-print fabric and mirrored for depth. At one end is a glass-enclosed fire for you to watch on winter evenings. Despite the rather feminine setting, dinners here are geared to masculine appetites, with straightforward stuff of the steak, prime rib, fried chicken genre. Lunch is another matter, with lots of light, wine-sauced and creamed casserole combinations as well as salads and cold platters. Worth mentioning is the consistently pleasant and efficient service.

THE HACIENDA, 36 West Mechanic Street, New Hope, Pennsylvania. Telephone: (215) 862-2078. Lunch: Tuesday-Thursday from 11:30. Dinner: Monday-Thursday 5-10:30; Saturday 5:30-11; Sunday 1-9. Cards: AE, DC, MC, VISA. Reservations advised. Full bar service. Free parking.

## Seafood Entrees

Seafood Casserole, a la Pamela w/wild _____ $7.95
Rice blend, Lobster, Shrimp, Scallops
and Crabmeat

10oz. Boneless Trout w/ Scallop Stuffing w/ _____ $9.95
wine cream caper sauce

Shrimp & Fresh Mushrooms Sauteed in _____ $8.50
wine & Butter, seasoned w/Herbs
and Garlic, w/wild Rice blend

Sauteed Scallops & Fresh Mushrooms _____ $7.95
in Casserole w/wild Rice blend

Deviled Crab Cake, a la Cadiz w/wine _____ $7.50
cream caper Sauce

Flounder a la Portugese · Fresh Flounder _____ $6.95
baked in a Mediterrean Tomato
Sauce in Casserole

Shrimp Scampi w/ lots of garlic _____ $7.95
Jumbo Fried Shrimp _____ $7.95
Fresh Fish of the day, deep fried or baked _____ $6.95
Sauteed Frogs Legs in wine and Garlic _____ $7.95
Butter on Toast

African Lobster Tails w/drawn butter
Price depends on size and current prices

## Meat Entrees

16oz. Hacienda's Sirloin Steak w/ onion Rings _____ $11.95

Surf & Turf, a 6oz. Filet Mignon w/ One 4oz. _____ $13.95
Lobster Tail

6oz. Petite Filet Mignon w/French Red Wine _____ $7.50
and Mushroom Sauce

9oz. Petite Filet Mignon w/French Red Wine _____ $10.50
and Mushroom Sauce

Prime Rib of Beef au Jus        Jr. Cut _____ $8.95
                          Executive Cut _____ $10.95

Filet Mignon Tips w/fresh mushrooms sauteed _____ $8.95
in Madeira Wine Sauce on bed of Wild Rice blend.

Beef a la Matador · Chunks of beef on a bed of _____ $7.95
green noodles in casserole w/Wine Mushroom Sauce

Baby Rack of Lamb for one w/Mint Jelly _____ $11.95

Veal Cordon Bleu, a la Pamela _____ $10.95

Veal and Mushrooms sauteed in Madeira Wine _____ $9.95

Baked Breast of Capon w/Gourmet Sauce _____ $6.95

Hacienda's Fried Chicken _____ $5.95

Chopped Sirloin Platter _____ $5.95

## Bucks County: New Hope Area
## HÔTEL DU VILLAGE
French                                    **$$**

The Hôtel du Village has the beamed ceilings, dark panel-
ing, detailed fireplaces and handsome hardwood floors of
an English manor house. Built as a private residence, it later
was transformed into a fashionable finishing school for
young ladies. Under the current owners, it is a decent,
though bar-less dining spot, where one feels a strong kinship
with the past. Classical music floats through the candelit
rooms. Waitresses with the manners and scrubbed faces of
country schoolgirls shyly serve you. The menu offers famil-
iar French fare and advises that birthday and special occa-
sion cakes will be provided with proper notice. Overnight
lodging is available on the property.

HÔTEL DU VILLAGE, North River Road and Phillips Mill
Road, New Hope area, Pennsylvania. Telephone: (215)
862-5164. Hours: Tuesday-Saturday from 5:30 pm; Sunday
from 3 pm. Cards: AE. Reservations advised. No alcoholic
beverages; bring your own wine. Free parking lot.

# Specialités de la Maison

**Tournedos Rossini**  8.95
(filet, wrapped with bacon, topped with paté, Perigourdine)

**Chateaubriand Bearnaise**  21.95
(for two)

**Entrecôte au Poivre**  8.95
(N.Y. sirloin, peppercorns, cream & brandy)

**Côtelettes d' Agneau Persillees**  8.95
(lamb chops with green herbs)

**Caneton Montmorency**  8.50
(duckling with cherries)

**Ris de Veau Financière**  8.50
(sweetbreads, green olives, mushrooms, Madeira)

**Médaillon de Veau Parisienne**  8.50
(veal medallion topped with a salpicon of chicken)

**Civet Villageois**  7.95
(a crust covered rabbit dish)

**Poulet Sauté a 'l' Algerienne**  7.50
(chicken in white wine, tomato, garlic)

# Les Poissons

**Les St. Jacques Provençales**  8.50
(scallops with garlic butter and tomato)

**Cuisses de Grenoville Fines Herbes**  7.95
(frogs legs, shallots, garlic, parsley butter and cream)

**Filets de Sole Richèlieu**  7.50
(sole in curried butter)

## Bucks County: Lahaska
## JENNY'S
## International $$

Jenny's is the Bucks County restaurant that dares depart from the accepted George Washington-slept-here style. The decor is New York nouveau, a manic marriage of merry-go-round and mirrors, softened with lovingly laundered table linens, fresh flowers and supremely comfortable chairs. At first Jenny's proudly proclaimed itself a purveyor of nouvelle cuisine, but lately, while specialties like rose petal soup still appear on the menu, there seems to be more emphasis on old standbys like steaks, rack of lamb and garlicky frogs legs. The restaurant takes late-evening dinner reservations without hesitation and should you feel frisky enough afterwards there's a glittery disco just up the stairs. Lunch is designed to make everyone happy. There are salads, sandwiches, omelets, crêpes, fish dishes, lamb chops and even a caviar mousse appetizer. There is, of course, a bar.

JENNY'S, The Yard, Lahaska, Pennsylvania. Telephone: (215) 794-5605. Lunch: Monday-Saturday from 11:30. Dinner: Tuesday-Saturday 5:30-11; Sunday from 4:30. Sunday brunch from 11 am. Cards: AE, MC, VISA. Reservations advised. Full bar service. Free parking lot.

# Specialties de la Nouvelle Cuisine

### Medallions de Veau Nouvelle
Lightly sauteed veal complimented by lobster and spinach
with a touch of Hollandaise

### Plume de Veau
Medallions of milk-fed veal sauteed in Sauce du Naturelle Cuisine

### Ris de Veau
~ discover how good sweetbreads really are

### Fruits de Mer
A fine selection of shellfish simmered in white wine and delicate
seasoning

### Chicken Valencia
Tender breast sauteed with orange and Cointreau

### Salmon de Cuisine
Fresh from the sea and enhanced with cucumber sauce

### Chicken Livers Stroganoff
A light saute enhanced with fresh mushrooms and Creme Fraiche

### Scallop-Shrimp Saute de Maison
Bay scallops and tender shrimp—an elegant saute

## Bucks County: Point Pleasant
## MOUNTAINSIDE INN
International

**$$**

Mountainside was a lot older-looking when we first found our way here about 10 years ago. The ancient building, typical of those early inns that front the River Road to New Hope, had stamped-tin ceilings, tiny cramped rooms and an air of trying very hard to please. The name and location remain the same, but the Mountainside we visited on a Saturday night not long ago was a lot like a friend who has lost 50 pounds, had her face lifted and her hair tinted. In the new Mountainside, walls of fake brick are paneled with mirrors. Identical tole lamps hang prettily over each white-clothed table. The rug underfoot has an Oriental pattern. A piano provides background music to wine and dine by. The conservative menu and wine list suit the clientele to a "T." An exciting appetizer here might be the fried mushrooms, which on our visit were sizzling and delicious, or a half-dozen clams buried under a flavorful casino blanket of vegetables and bacon. The house salad dressing is a tasty, garlic-cheese blend. Dinner entrées present a choice of steaks, beef Wellington, chicken Kiev, duckling, flounder, veal, liver or sweetbreads. For lunch the restaurant offers some interesting egg dishes, including a crab imperial omelet, as well as salads, seafood and kabobs. Desserts for both meals include Ponchartrain pie, high and handsome and, for chocolate freaks, a pear with hot fudge sauce.

MOUNTAINSIDE INN, River Road (Route 32), Point Pleasant, Pennsylvania. Telephone: (215) 297-5722. Lunch: Monday-Saturday 11 am-4 pm. Dinner: Monday-Thursday 5 pm-10 pm; Friday and Saturday 5 pm-11 pm. Cards: AE, DC, MC (tips may not be charged). Full bar service. Free parking.

# Mountainside Inn

## APPETIZERS

Clams Casino  3.95

Chicken Liver Paté  1.95

Oysters Rockefeller  4.25
(in season)

French Fried Mushrooms  1.95

Oysters on the Half Shell  3.95
(in season)

Escargot à la Bourgingnonne  4.25

Caviar and Hard-Boiled Egg  6.75
with Chilled Vodka

Coquilles Saint Jacques  4.95

Herring in Sour Cream  3.50

Asperges en Croûte  2.95

Cherrystone Clams  3.95
on the Half Shell

## SOUPS

Baked Onion Soup Gratineé  1.95

Onion Soup Natural  1.50
with Parmesan Cheese

Vichyssoise  1.75

HOUSE SALAD à la carte  1.75

Garlic Bread  1.50

## DINNER ENTREES

BROILED BONELESS SIRLOIN STEAK  16.95
With Bearnaise Sauce

BROILED BONELESS SIRLOIN STEAK  14.95
with Teriyaki Sauce

BROILED FILET MIGNON  15.95
with Bearnaise Sauce

BEEF WELLINGTON with Brandied Mushroom Sauce  19.95

BAKED BREAST OF CHICKEN KIEV  8.95
with Bigarade Sauce

BRANDIED BREAST OF CHICKEN  8.95
with Sauteed Vegetables in Wine Sauce

ROAST DUCKLING with Bigarade or Cumberland Sauce  10.95

SEAFOOD COQUELLES  10.95

SHRIMP SCAMPI on Saffron Rice  11.95

BAKED FILET OF FLOUNDER with Crab Imperial Stuffing  10.95

VEAL FLORENTINE  11.95

VEAL CORDON BLEU  11.95

VEAL PICCATA  10.95

SAUTEED CALVES' LIVER  9.95
with Bacon or Onions

SAUTEED SWEETBREADS  9.95
with Mushrooms

## Bucks County: Quakertown
## SIGN OF THE SORREL HORSE
French                                          **$$**

There is a certain type of restaurant diner who will not be impressed by the Sorrel Horse. The place is too quietly competent. There are no decor distractions. The menu is brief and the selections spelled out plainly. There is another type of restaurant diner who will realize that all of the above indicates that the food here is good enough to stand up to the glare of the spotlight. Here are some examples from one visit to the inn: stuffed mushrooms heaped high with bits of fragrant pork sausage; extraordinary house salad with greens, mushrooms, shrimp pieces and a tangy buttermilk dressing; vol au vent of lobster in excellent made-here puff pastry; chicken stuffed with lemon and crushed walnuts; brie with an exquisitely ripe pear; frozen lemon cream served in the lemon shell with a fresh orange blossom for accent. A more recent menu shows an emphasis on daily specialties dictated by seasonal bounty and market availability. A small but carefully selected wine list offers drinkable wines at reasonable prices. The inn is located in the quiet countryside of the Quakertown area, and if that means a two-hour drive from where you live, consider overnight lodging; a few rooms are available.

**SIGN OF THE SORREL HORSE, Old Bethlehem Road, Quakertown, Pennsylvania. Telephone: (215) 536-4651. Lunch: Tuesday-Saturday 11:30-2. Dinner: Tuesday-Sunday from 5:30. Closed Monday. Cards: AE, MC, VISA. Reservations advised. Full bar service. Free parking.**

## Soups

Soup du Jour                                  1.50
Bisque à la Maison                            1.75

## Appetizers

House Salad                                   1.75
Escargots en Champignon                       3.75
Pate                                          2.25
Oysters Baton Rouge                           2.75

## Entrees

Curried Chicken w/ Almonds                    8.25
Poisson du Jour                               7.50
Veal du Jour                                  8.50
Stuffed Medallions of Pork                    8.25
Tournedos                                    10.75
Scallops and Shrimp à la Parisienne           9.00
Quail w/ Grapes and Cognac                    9.50

# Chester County

# Chester County: Devon
# CHINESE DELIGHT
Chinese                                              $

If the friendly folks at Chinese Delight don't like kids, their
job of pretending is good enough to win an Oscar. One
chilly evening, four muffled and mittened youngsters, none
taller than their parents' belt buckles, blinked their way
into the bright dining room and rated more attention than
Mayor Rizzo at the Ninth Street market. Two additional
families of six arrived minutes later and met with the same
treatment. The pats and smiles splashed the kids with
affection the way most of us splash soy sauce on fried rice.
The dazzled small fry responded by behaving better than
adults. Many of those crowding the restaurant seem to have
discovered Chinese Delight when it was a tiny take out place
and as a result they continue to order standard take-out
items, overlooking the menu's more adventurous possibil-
ities like hacked chicken (firm, julienne strips of cold chick-
en in a sauce dominated by the flavors of sesame and soy),
abalone and chicken soup, whole steamed fish, shredded
pork with Szechwan sauce. I don't often recommend desserts in a Chinese restaurant, but I heartily endorse the
honeyed banana here, meltingly soft banana segments en-
cased in chewy caramel. The fritters arrive hot then are
plunged into ice water tableside for a little dining excitement.

CHINESE DELIGHT, 735 Lancaster Avenue, Devon, Pennsylvania. Telephone: (215) 687-1866. Hours: Monday-Saturday 11 am-11 pm; closed Sunday. No cards. No liquor
license. Bring your own wine. Free parking.

## Chester County: Paoli
## BUOY 1
## Seafood $

Supermarket-style display cases are the brightest elements in the decor of this family-owned seafood shop and restaurant. Walls are painted cinder block; plates are paper; "silver" is plastic. To order, step up to the counter, pay in advance for your choice and get a clam shell with your number painted on it. Wait until the food is prepared to order (watch if you'd like) and one of the young waiters or waitresses yells your number, finds you and brings the food to you at your varnished picnic table. So what's the big holler about Buoy 1? No question in anyone's mind. The place serves up nicely cooked fresh fish and shellfish at prices lower than most of us could duplicate at home. The daily special ($1 at this writing but I can't believe even Buoy 1 can fight inflation much longer) is fried fish of the day plus French fries and a choice of one of a large variety of homemade deli-type salads (or you can select two salads instead). The fish varies but the portion size is always decent, the breading is always the lightest veil and the fish itself always tastes fresh. If you don't crave the special, there are good buys on fish chowder (the kind of chowder changes daily with the catch), fishcakes, fried shellfish, sandwiches, even broiled fish or shellfish, which Buoy 1 obligingly offers with butter, cheese sauce or, for those on restricted diets, plain. The place lacks a liquor license but you're invited to bring your own beer or wine. If you'd rather dine at home, the entire menu is available for take out. There's also a retail counter where seafood is for sale uncooked or ready-to-cook.

BUOY 1, Lancaster Pike (Route 30), between Paoli and Malvern, Pennsylvania. Telephone: (215) 644-0549. Hours: daily 11 am-9 pm. No cards. No reservations. No alcoholic beverages. Bring your own wine or beer. Free parking.

# BUOY APPETIZERS

| | |
|---|---|
| Crabmeat Cocktail | 3.00 |
| Shrimp Cocktail 1 Doz. | 3.00 |
| 4 Oysters on ½ Shell | 1.00 |
| Showboat | 3.00 |
| (4 oysters/4 clams/4 shrimp) | |
| 4 Clams on ½ Shell | 1.00 |
| Onion Rings | 1.00 |
| Chowder | .50 |

# BUOY FRIED
### (Pick One Plus Two)

| | |
|---|---|
| Stuffed Shrimp | 4.50 |
| Combo | 4.00 |
| Shrimp | 3.50 |
| Oysters | 3.50 |
| Scallops | 3.50 |
| Chicken ½ | 2.50 |
| New England Clams | 2.50 |
| Flounder | 2.00 |
| Fish Cakes | 1.50 |
| Fish Du Jour | 1.00 |

# BUOY BROIL'S
### (Pick One Plus Two)

| | |
|---|---|
| Crab Mornay | 4.50 |
| Scallops | 4.50 |
| Flounder | 3.50 |
| Fish Du Jour | 3.00 |

# BUOY SANDWICH
### (Served on Bun Only)

| | |
|---|---|
| Crab Cake | 2.50 |
| Shrimp Salad | 2.00 |
| Chicken Salad | 1.50 |
| Flounder | 1.50 |
| Oyster | 1.50 |
| Fish Cake | 1.00 |
| Fish w/Sauce | 1.00 |
| Egg Salad | 1.00 |

# Chester County: Phoenixville
# COLUMBIA HOTEL
## American

**$$**

How do you feel about a dining room where, on a Saturday night, only the waiters look really dressed up? Where the table space is shared by a bar and dinner music is partly the sound coming from a big color TV set over that bar? Where everyone seems to know everyone else yet somehow you don't feel left out? You'd like it? Then you're ripe for a visit to the Columbia, that gem in downtown Phoenixville, the town that steel built. The Columbia has four dining rooms, but the bar, with its polished wood and gaslight globes, seems the coziest ... the "in" place to dine. Fresh, whole Maine lobster is an ongoing special at the hotel. The lobsters are available steamed and buttery or, if you'd rather steam your own, live to take home. Tuesday is the big night for beef-eaters. That's when the Columbia offers a 15-ounce New York strip steak for $7.95. Prime rib in three sizes, from large to gargantuan, is available on the weekend. The hotel has a children's menu that features lobster tail in addition to the usual kiddie fare. The wine list is small but very interesting.

COLUMBIA HOTEL, 148 Bridge Street, Phoenixville, Pennsylvania. Telephone: (215) 933-9973. Lunch: Monday-Saturday 11:30-3. Dinner: Monday-Saturday 4-10; Sunday 3:30-8:30. Cards: AE, DC, VISA. Reservations recommended on the weekend. Full service bar. Parking lot.

# Appetizers

| | | | |
|---|---|---|---|
| Cocktail of Seasonal Fruit with Sherbet | .95 | Mushrooms Stuffed with Crab Imperial | 3.75 |
| Chilled Tomato, Grapefruit or Orange Juice | .30 | Clams Casino (6) | 3.25 |
| Iced Cherrystone Clams .... (6) 1.75 .... (12) 3.50 | | Dozen Steamed Topneck Clams | 2.75 |
| Jumbo White Panamanian Shrimp Cocktail (4) | 4.00 | Escargots | 3.25 |
| Scampi a la Maison (3) | | 5.00 | |

# Soups

| | Columbia Snapper Soup | | | | Homemade Soup du Jour | | |
|---|---|---|---|---|---|---|---|
| Cup | 1.00 | Bowl | 1.50 | Cup | .75 | Bowl | 1.25 |

# Entrees

**BONELESS BROILED BROOK TROUT** — *Broiled to perfection, served with drawn butter*     8.50

**CRABMEAT CASSEROLE** — *Baked Alaskan king crab meat, sea scallops and gulf shrimp
mixed in a delicate white cream sauce, flavored with chablis and topped with grated cheese —
served en casserole with toast points*     A Specialty of the Hotel   8.75

**THE SWEET TENDER MEAT OF THE ALASKAN KING CRAB LEG** —
*Carefully sauteed and served on a rice pilaf with drawn butter*     11.95

**VEAL CUTLET PARMIGIANA** — *A tender cutlet of veal deep fried,
smothered in mozarella cheese and topped with our own tomato sauce*     5.95

**BROILED FLOUNDER** — *A fresh filet of flounder broiled to your specifications
and served with drawn butter*     7.95

**GOLDEN FRIED JUMBO WHITE PANAMANIAN SHRIMP (3)** —
*The famous white shrimp of Panama, cleaned, butterflied and breaded in our kitchen,
deepfried and served with our own cocktail sauce or tartar sauce*     7.50

**PETITE FILET MIGNON** — *A fine center cut filet broiled to your order, served on toast,
accompanied with our own mushroom sauce and topped with a juicy steak mushroom*     6.75

**STUFFED SCALLOPS** — *Tender bay scallops mixed with Alaskan king crab meat and gulf shrimp
in our own white sauce, served on a bed of melted cheese en casserole*     A Specialty of the Hotel   8.95

**CRAB IMPERIAL** – *We use the finest fresh lump backfin crabmeat in our recipe
and serve it on a scallop shell topped with mayonnaise*     8.95

**MUSHROOMS STUFFED WITH CRAB IMPERIAL** — *Fresh Kennet Square "specials"
stuffed with our own fresh backfin crab imperial*     8.95

**PRIME NEW YORK STRIP STEAKS** — *The finest center cuts of the strip
broiled to your specifications and topped with a juicy steak mushroom*

| | | |
|---|---|---|
| | 10 Ounce | 7.75 |
| | 15 Ounce | 9.50 |
| *Pittsburgh or garlic and black pepper crust available upon request* | 18 Ounce | 12.25 |

**STUFFED TROUT** — *A boneless brook trout stuffed with our
backfin crab imperial and served with drawn butter*     9.50

**SCAMPI A LA MAISON** — *The famous white shrimp of Panama, butterflied and
carefully sauteed in our special scampi sauce, served on a bed of rice*     A Specialty of the Hotel   8.95

**TWIN PETITE FILETS** – *Two of our finest center cut filets broiled to your order,
served on toast, accompanied with our mushroom sauce and topped with juicy steak mushrooms*     11.95

**STUFFED FLOUNDER** — *A filet of flounder stuffed with crabmeat, scallops and shrimp,
served with a border of dutchess potatoes*     8.95

**ALASKAN KING CRAB LEGS** — *The tasty legs of the Alaskan king crab
steamed to a tender readiness, served with drawn butter*     9.95

**ROCK LOBSTER TAIL** — *The tail of the famous cold water rock lobster,
first baked and then finished under the broiler, served with drawn butter*     Priced according to weight

**THE COLUMBIA**   *A fine center cut petite filet, accompanied by a generous
portion of steamed Alaskan king crab legs, served with drawn butter*     11.50

**THE GASLIGHT** – *A cold water rock lobster tail accompanied by
a center cut petite filet, served with drawn butter*     12.50

**FRESH WHOLE MAINE LOBSTERS**   *The, not to be duplicated, king of the North Atlantic,
picked from our salt water tanks in our Lobster Shoppe and served to you perfectly
steamed with drawn butter*     A Specialty of the Hotel     Priced according to weight

## Chester County: Coventryville
## COVENTRY FORGE INN
### French

**$$**

The cover of the current Coventry Forge menu shows a nonchalantly naked Lady Godiva astride a grazing steed. Like the lady, Coventry Forge has been doing its own thing for some time now (25 years, actually) and isn't about to be distracted by the roar of the crowd. The food here is so simply stated that anyone with a palate tuned to less subtle seasoning is best forewarned to go elsewhere. Truite au bleu in beurre blanc, a personal favorite from the menu, is nothing more than a handsome local trout kept alive until the very last second before poaching, then delicately cloaked in a silken butter sauce. Steak au poivre has never been more than a thick slice of rare, tender beef in a sauce made piquant with green peppercorns. A spinach timbale, one of the memorable vegetable offerings, contains a core of perfect, fresh mushroom slices. Desserts include home-made ice cream and sorbet, fresh-baked pastries and, when the season is right, luscious raspberries from a neighboring farm. The wine selection reflects the owner's expertise in that area. Coventry Forge was built in 1717 and has been beautifully restored and maintained. A glass-enclosed porch is a lovely place to dine in summer when there's a sunset to savor. Smaller, inside dining rooms are cozy on chilly days. Recently, owners June and Wallis Callahan responded to requests of guests who travel great distances to reach the restaurant and have furnished a luxurious guest house that offers large rooms and baths and a serene country view. Price of a room includes Continental breakfast on the porch of the inn.

COVENTRY FORGE INN, Route 23, Coventryville, Pennsylvania. Telephone: (215) 469-6222. Hours: Tuesday-Friday 5:30 pm-9 pm; Saturday 5:30 pm-10 pm (prix fixe menu on Saturday). No cards. Reservations essential. Full bar service. Free parking.

Potages

Soupe à l'Oignon Gratinée    2.75
Crème de Cresson    2.00
Crème Vichyssoise    2.00


Hors d'Oeuvres

Feuilleté d'Escargots Champenoise    4.50
Pâté du Chef    3.00
Coquilles Saint-Jacques à la Parisienne    3.95
Avocat aux Fruits de Mer    3.75
Saumon Troisgros    3.95
Artichaut Vinaigrette    2.50
Ratatouille    2.50
Ecrevisses du Domaine à la Nage    4.90
Truite au Bleu, Sauce Beurre Blanc    4.75


Entrees

Canard à l'Orange    9.00
Steak au Poivre    12.50
Supreme de Canard Grillé, pour 2 pers.    20.00
Rognon de Veau, Sauce Moutarde    7.50
Sirloin Steak, Beurre Maitre d'Hotel    14.00
Ris de Veau au Madère    9.50
Suprème de Volaille en Croûte, Sauce Perigorde    8.50
Escalopes de Veau à la Crème    10.00
Carré d'Agneau Rôti    15.00
Foie de Veau au Persil    8.50
Crabe Wallis    8.75
Poitrine de Veau    8.50


Entremets

Crème Caramel Renversée    1.50          Mousse au Chocolat    1.75
Baba au Rhum    2.00               Profiteroles Glacé    2.00
Les Trois Sorbets    1.75               Fraises    2.50
Gateau de Fromage    1.75               Fromage    2.50
Framboises    2.75                    Pêche Melba    2.25
Glacé Vanille à la Philadelphie    1.75


Café    1.00               Thé    1.00
Café Filtre, Pot    1.00

### Chester Country: West Chester
### DILWORTHTOWN INN
### Continental

**$$**

For the sake of authenticity, this 18th-century dwelling was left with its family-sized rooms intact when it was converted to a restaurant in 1972. Whether you love, like or run from this attractive restoration could just hinge on how you feel about dining in a room so small that anything spoken above a whisper immediately becomes semi-public. The nearness of your roommates could, of course, prove a boon if they're attractive folks engrossed in their own small talk. For those who would rather eat than eavesdrop, the Dilworthtown menu obliges with several pages of specialties. Whole English sole meunière is usually a good choice. The fish is cooked in butter, then skillfully boned at tableside. Tempting, too, is the duckling stuffed with wild rice and chestnuts and sauced with peach nectar. For the area's country squires or the business groups that drift in from nearby Wilmington, there are steaks, filet mignon, and on weekends, a slab of prime rib. Desserts include an impressive baked Alaska for two or four. The wine list is better than average.

DILWORTHTOWN INN, 1/4 mile off Route 202, outside of West Chester, Pennsylvania. Telephone: (215) 399-1390. Hours: Monday-Saturday 5:30-10:30 pm; Sunday 3-9 pm. Cards: AE, DC, MC, VISA. Reservations advised. Full bar service. Free parking.

**ST. JACQUES EN COCOTTE** ..................... 10.25
*Tender Bay Scallops and Fresh Mushrooms Embraced in*
*A Light Wine and Cream Sauce Gratinee to a*
*Golden Brown*

**LES CREVETTES PROVENCALE (Shrimp Scampi)** ............ 10.25
*Colossal Scampis Sauteed in Lemon and Garlic Butter,*
*Flambeed in Cognac and Served with Italian Risotto*

**CRAB IMPERIAL** ..................... 10.50
*Lump Crabmeat Baked in Casserole*

**SOUTH AFRICAN LOBSTER TAILS** .................... 13.95
*Drawn Butter*

**LE CHATEAUBRIAND BEARNAISE (For Two)** .............. 25.50
*Medium-Rare At It's Best. Jardiniere of Garden Fresh*
*Vegetables, Provencale Tomatoes and Bearnaise Sauce*

**LE CARRE D'AGNEAU PERSILLADE (For Two)** .............. 25.00
*A Rack of Lamb, Marinated in Brandy and Rosemary,*
*Roasted and Topped with Mustard, Special Blend*
*of Herbes Provencales*

**LE BOEUF WELLINGTON (For Two)** ..................... 27.00
*A Filet of Beef, Fourre with Pate de Foie Gras,*
*Surrounded with Mushrooms and Baked in a Pastry*
*Dough, Served with Sauce Perigueux*

**LE STEAK AU POIVRE** .....................12.75
*A Tender 14 oz. Sirloin Steak, Laced with Crushed*
*Peppercorns and Flambeed At Your Table, Topped with*
*A Sauce Made of Veal Glaze and Heavy Cream*

**LES MEDALLIONS DE VEAU Aux Champignons** ............ 11.75
*Tender Medallions of Milk Fed Veal, Sauteed in Butter,*
*Garnished with Fresh Picked Mushrooms and Served*
*with Dry Vermouth Cream Sauce*

**FILET MIGNON TID BITS** .....................10.50
*with Mushrooms and Sauce Bordelaise*

## Chester County: St. Peters
## THE INN AT ST. PETERS
### International

$$

The deck attached to this vintage inn lofts you into the treetops, over a stream bed in which a herd of buffalo-sized boulders seem frozen forever in stampede formation. On a lovely day it's a fine view as you sip your cocktail somewhat removed from the tourist bustle of this restored, paintbox-pretty village of shops. Given less than ideal weather, however, and you'll do better at a cozy table inside where, if you're lucky, you'll get much of the same scenery in comfort. Worth noting is the especially cordial treatment of couples. Twosomes are given attractive windowside tables rather than the dark corner or kitchen-door spots they rate in many other foursome-minded restaurants. Service tends to be smiling rather than polished, and that probably stems from the inn's rather remote location. The food is basic but with some nice touches. The kitchen does well on clams casino and snapper soup and lump crabmeat au gratin. The lemon and dill house salad dressing is another treat.

THE INN AT ST. PETERS, Village of St. Peters, Pennsylvania. Telephone: (215) 469-6277. Lunch: Tuesday-Saturday 11:30-2:30. Dinner: Tuesday-Thursday 5-9; Friday and Saturday to 10:30; Sunday 1-7. Cards: AE, MC, VISA. Reservations advised. Full bar service. Parking lot. German oompah band Sunday afternoon 1:30-5:30.

## Chester County: Phoenixville Area
## KIMBERTON INN
## AND COUNTRY HOUSE
International $$

Several managements have come and gone since we discovered the Kimberton Country House years ago, but based on current dining experience, none has done better by the place than the present crowd. That's good news because the large, attractively decorated restaurant with its colonial-costumed waitresses has always been a handsome setting for meals. Scoops of creamy cheese spread arrive with crackers for cocktail snacking. Bread and rolls are baked here and are so tempting that if you aren't careful your appetite will be done in by the preliminaries. Save room for such goodies, however, as the well-made beef Wellington and oysters Chesapeake. The latter are baked with crabmeat in a deliciously rich sauce. The resident baker provides home-made cheesecake and pies for dessert. Because the restaurant is located in a scenic rural area and has windows to take advantage of the view, it's a popular lunch spot. The luncheon menu is large, ranging from salads and sandwiches to hot entrées like an out-of-the-ordinary Viennese lemon chicken marinated in herbs and lemon juice and sautéed in butter.

KIMBERTON INN AND COUNTRY HOUSE, just off Route 113, near Phoenixville, Pennsylvania. Telephone: (215) 933-8148. Lunch: Tuesday-Saturday 11:30 am-2:30 pm. Dinner: Tuesday-Friday 5 pm-10 pm; Saturday 5 pm-11 pm; Sunday 1 pm-9 pm. Cards: AE, DC, MC, VISA. Full bar service. Parking lot. Children's menu.

## Chester County: West Chester
## LA COCOTTE
French                                            $$

You'd expect to find luncheonettes on the main street of this rather typical college town. La Cocotte is definitely not a luncheonette. It is a caring French restaurant with cuisine that is more classique than nouvelle and prices that pay for kitchen talent and expensive ingredients rather than location or decor. Find the menu filled with familiar favorites like onion soup, pâté maison, escargots, mousse au chocolat, crème caramel. The truite is either aux amandes or meunière. The sole is with crème. Canard is orange glazed and the poulet is avec estragon. It's all done with style and friendliness. There's wine of the same high quality as the food and a nice little bar up front. If you aren't familiar with the West Chester area, allow yourself some extra time to savor this pretty town's tree-lined streets and handsome old homes.

LA COCOTTE, 124 West Gay Street, West Chester, Pennsylvania. Telephone: (215) 436-6722. Lunch: Monday-Friday 11:30-2. Dinner: Monday-Saturday 6-9:30; closed Sunday. Cards: AE, MC, VISA. Reservations advised. Full bar service. Municipal parking.

### Potages
soupe du jour 1.25
soupe a l'oignon 2.25
creme de champignon 2.00

### Hor D'Oeuvres
#### froids
paté maison 2.75
salade au crabe 4.75

#### chauds
escargots de bourgogne 3.75
crepes au fruits de mer 4.00
quiche au poireaux 2.75

### Poissons
poisson du jour
truite aux amandes ou meuniere 8.50

filets de sole à la crème 8.00
scampis provençale 8.25

### Volailles
canard a l'orange 8.75

faisan aux légumes 9.00
poulet cocotte a l'estragon 8.50

### Veau et Agneau
escaloppe de veau au crabe 9.75

cote d'agneau grillé 9.50
carré d'agneau pour deux 21.00

### Boeuf
steak au poivre 9.75
tournedos rossini ou henri IV 10.50

emincé de boeuf 8.50
chateaubriand pour deux 21.50

salad and vegetables are included with your dinner

### Les Desserts
mousse au chocolat 2.00
crème au caramel 1.75
poires au pernod pour deux 4.50

fraises au grand marnier 2.25
pêches melba 2.00
baked alaska pour deux 5.00

## Chester County: Mendenhall
## MENDENHALL INN
### American/Continental

**$$**

The floral wonders of Longwood Gardens, the American furniture treasures of Winterthur, the historic battlefields of Brandywine, along with the nostalgic country scenes that inspired the Wyeth family, all annually draw countless visitors to Mendenhall's neighborhood. For many, the pleasures of the day are crowned by a meal at this attractive inn. The Mendenhall Inn does its best to live up to the high standards set by the area. I'm remembering the coronation melon with which I began one review meal here—a large wedge of sweet, perfectly ripe melon embellished with crown jewels of perfect grapes, a sparkling orange slice and a strawberry as big as the Ritz. Chincoteague oysters on the half shell were icily regal, their shells lounging royally on a white, indented oyster plate. Salads were bounteous and dressed, at our waitress' suggestion, in an ermine wrap of blue cheese and cream that would have cost extra almost anywhere else. A calves liver sauté was two thin, perfectly

## APPETIZERS AND HORS D'OEUVRES

Pâté of Fresh Chicken Livers   **2.75**

Cherrystone Clams, *Casino*   **3.50**      Cherrystone Clams *on the* Half Shell   **2.25**

Chincoteague Oysters *on the* Half Shell   **3.25**

Coronation Melon Wedge   **2.75**      Escargots Bourguignonne   **4.50**

Fresh Orange Sections *in* Champagne   **2.75**

Kennett Square Mushrooms      Jumbo Panamanian Shrimp
*stuffed with* Crabmeat   **4.50**      Cocktail, *Cocktail Sauce*   **4.50**

ROMANOFF BELUGA CAVIAR
one ounce
**17.50** *(for two)*

## ❧ SOUPS ❧

Baked French Onion Soup, *Gratinée*   **1.75**

Philadelphia Snapper Soup   **1.25**      Soup *du* Jour   **1.00**

Caesar Salad, *(for two)*   **4.75**

cooked slices topped with slivers of good Canadian bacon. Double loin lamb chops were pink and perfect under a well-seared exterior. Even the desserts rated raves. Fresh strawberries with heavy cream arrived happily sloshed in wine. The nectarine Melba boasted rich ice cream and faintly tart raspberry purée. The Mendenhall wine list has a good selection of American and imported wines at affordable (under $10 a bottle) prices as well as some more expensive, exceptional vintages. A barn built in 1796 is a part of the inn and the lower floor of an ancient mill is now the main dining room. There are several working fireplaces; one of which greets you in the lobby with a warm glow (in the appropriate season, of course.)

MENDENHALL INN, Kennet Pike, Village of Mendenhall, Pennsylvania. Telephone: (215) 388-1181. Lunch: Tuesday-Saturday 11:30-2:30. Dinner: Tuesday-Thursday 5-10:30; Friday and Saturday 5-midnight; Sunday 3-8. Cards: AE, DC, MC, VISA. Reservations advised. Full bar service. Free parking.

---

## ~ ENTRÉES ~

*Served with your entrées are salad, your choice of dressing and two vegetables of the day.*

**BROILED FILET OF SOLE,** *Amandine* **7.75**

**BONELESS BROOK TROUT** *stuffed with* **LUMP CRABMEAT 9.50**

**BROILED SOUTH AFRICAN LOBSTER TAILS** *with Drawn Butter* **14.50**

**LUMP CRABMEAT IMPERIAL,** *Mendenhall* **9.50**

**BAKED STUFFED FLOUNDER,** *with* **CRABMEAT 9.50**

**BAKED STUFFED OYSTERS** *with* **LUMP CRABMEAT 9.50**

**BROILED HALF SPRING CHICKEN 7.50**

**CALF'S LIVER SAUTÉ,** *Canadian Bacon* **9.25**

**CENTER CUT DOUBLE LOIN LAMB CHOPS,** *Mint Jelly* **11.75**

**ASSORTED SEAFOOD PLATE 11.50**

**FILET MIGNON,** *Mushroom Cap* **11.50**

**NEW YORK STRIP SIRLOIN,** *One Pound, Mushroom Cap* **11.50**

**ROAST PRIME RIB of WESTERN BEEF,** *au Jus* **10.75**

**TENDERLOIN OF BEEF EN BROCHETTE,** *Seasoned Rice* **8.75**

**A PETITE FILET MIGNON** *and* **SOUTH AFRICAN LOBSTER TAIL 13.50**

Sautéed Mushrooms, *Mendenhall* **2.25**     Fried Bermuda Onion Rings **2.25**

## SEAFOOD SHANTY
**Seafood**                                    **$$**

Seafood Shanty restaurants abound locally. The chain's rapid growth is no accident. What is offered here is good-quality seafood at prices that are noticeably lower than most other seafood restaurants can afford to charge. "The secret to our low prices is volume," says one local Shanty manager. The menu is so large, and has so many different comfinations of broiled, fried and steamed seafood, that it may be difficult to make a selection. One steamed combination is composed of tiny perfect clams, oysters, lobster tail, shrimp and king crab legs, steamed just long enough to cook them and release the mollusks from their shells. An order of shrimp stuffed with crabmeat proved to be an ample serving of the former bedded in the latter. Desserts are not an afterthought as might be expected at a seafood restaurant. A strawberry tart sampled had a delicious, fresh berry filling and fork-tender pastry. There's a big, busy bar and lounge area where, unless you arrive at an unusually quiet hour, you'll get to wait for a table. Oh yes, there's a special children's menu, too.

SEAFOOD SHANTY, locations throughout the Philadelphia area. Restaurants reviewed at Lancaster Pike in Paoli, and Roosevelt Boulevard and Cottman Avenue in Philadelphia, Pennsylvania. Telephone: Paoli restaurant, (215) 647-1500. Hours: daily 11 am-midnight. Cards: AE, DC, MC, VISA. No reservations. Full bar service. Free parking.

# World's Best Fish and Chips
## 4.50

## Stuffed Flounder

Fresh Fillets Loaded with Crabmeat
A Gourmets Delight . . . . . . . . . . . . . . . . 7.95

## Stuffed Shrimp

Four Shrimp overstuffed and baked with
Our Secret Crabmeat Stuffing . . . . . . . . . 7.95

## Hot Seafood Feast

Steamed Lobster Tail, Clams, Shrimp,
Oysters, King Crab and Mussels . . . . . . . 11.95

## Cold Seafood Feast

Cold Lobster Tail, Clams, Shrimp
Oysters & King Crab . . . . . . . . . . . . . . . .10.95

## Chester County: Phoenixville
## SEVEN STARS INN
## American

**$$**

Excess is not accidental at this rural Phoenixville restaurant. It's planned and it's a major part of the place's considerable appeal. Order the roast prime rib and it's almost a certainty that you will tote home enough for sandwiches and snacks. Order crab imperial and a mountain of crab arrives. Other portions, including vegetables and salads, are also slightly larger than life size, and the surprise is that everything tastes fresh and carefully prepared. With one exception everything sampled has received uniformly high marks, and that includes spicy, thick snapper soup and an unusual chilled, chopped roast beef appetizer served with horse-radish sauce. The rib is prime, cooked as ordered and overwhelming in size. The crab imperial is a trifle bready, but it is nicely seasoned and the pieces of crabmeat are large and delicious. Vegetables are crisp-cooked broccoli, cucumbers in cream, terrific French fries and good fried eggplant. That exception? A strawberry cheesecake dessert that was totally bland. But then who needs dessert after all that? From a decorator's point of view the Seven Stars is a hodgepodge that tries, without much luck, to blend Victorian flocked wallcoverings and carved, damask chairs with barn beams and siding. But I doubt that most of the Seven Stars patrons notice. They're too busy studying the long menu. Or eating. And eating. And eating.

SEVEN STARS INN, Ridge Road, Route 23, Phoenixville, Pennsylvania. Telephone: (215) 495-5205. Hours: Tuesday-Friday 5-10; Saturday 4:30-11. Closed Sunday and Monday. No cards. Reservations required on Saturday. Full bar service. Parking lot. Children's menu.

## *Entrees*

ALL ENTREES INCLUDE
TOSSED FRESH GARDEN SALAD WITH YOUR CHOICE OF DRESSING
FRENCH    RUSSIAN    ITALIAN    ROQUEFORT (.60 Extra)
FRESH ASSORTED DINNER ROLLS
CHEDDAR CHEESE AND CRACKERS COMPLIMENTS OF HISTORIAL SEVEN STARS INN

## *Prime Beef and Meat Entrees*

WE SERVE ONLY TOP QUALITY WESTERN USDA GRADE PRIME BEEF AND MEATS

YE-OLDE-INN SPECIALTY              (NO-SUBSTITUTES)           PLATTER

**ROAST WESTERN PRIME RIBS OF BEEF AU JUS**
The King's Extra Cut of Slow Roasted Prime Beef, As You Like It . . . . 13.95
BIN NO. 12

**BROILED PRIME FILET MIGNON (16 oz. or More) (Deluxe Cut)**
French Fried Onion Rings . . . . . . . . . . . . . . . . 13.95
BIN NO. 10 OR 21

**BROILED PRIME SIRLOIN STEAK (24-oz. or More) (Cattleman Cut)**
French Fried Onion Rings . . . . . . . . . . . . . . . . 13.95
BIN NO. 11 OR 23

**SAUTEED FRESH CALF'S LIVER** with Bacon or Onion Rings . . . . . . . 9.95
BIN NO. 20 OR 40

ALL VEAL DISHES SERVED WITH SIDE OF FETTUCCINE

**GOLDEN BROWN TENDER BREADED MILK-FED WHITE VEAL CUTLET**
Served on a Bed of Tomato Sauce . . . . . . . . . . . . . 9.50
BIN NO. 35

**SAUTEED CALF'S VEAL SWEETBREADS** (Mushrooms) Sause Bordeaux . . . . 10.95
**SCALLOPINE OF VEAL** (Marsala Wine) . . . . . . . . . . . . 9.95
BIN NO. 30 OR 40

**SAUTEED VEAL KIDNEYS AND MUSHROOMS,** Maderia Wine Sauce . . . . 8.95

**NATURE PRIMO WHITE VEAL PARMEGIANA**
Imported Mozzarella Cheese, Rich Tomato Sauce . . . . . . . . 9.95
BIN NO. 25 OR 43

**VEAL A LA SEVEN STARS** Tender Pieces of Milk Fed Veal Sauteed in Butter
with Mushrooms and Wine Sauce, Topped with Prosciutto and Imported
Mozzarella Cheese—Baked in Oven until Golden Brown . . . . . . 10.50
BIN NO. 25

**VEAL A LA FRANCAISE** with Fettuccine . . . . . . . . . . . . 10.50
BIN NO. 11 OR 21

**SAUTEED BREAST OF CAPON CORDON BLEU**
Filled with Ham and Cheese with Wine Sauce . . . . . . . . . 8.95

## *Seafood Entrees*

**A LA SEVEN STARS SHRIMP SALAD PLATTER** . . . . . . . . 9.95

**BROILED SOUTH AFRICAN LOBSTER TAIL — DRAWN BUTTER**
18 oz.'s or More—Seasoned and Finished Under Gleaming Embers—
Tender and Delicious . . . . . . . . . . . . . . . . _____
BIN NO. 36 OR 40

**BAKED BACKFIN CRABMEAT IMPERIAL — ALL LUMP CRABMEAT** . . 9.95
BIN NO. 35

**BAKED JUMBO STUFFED SHRIMP IMPERIAL** with Crabmeat . . . . 10.95

**SAUTEED FRESH JUMBO SHRIMP SCAMPI** Ala 7 Stars . . . . . 10.95

**SAUTEED FRESH JUMBO SHRIMP** with Rice Pilaf . . . . . . 10.95
BIN NO. 33 OR 41

**BROILED FILET OF ATLANTIC FLOUNDER** — Stuffed with Imperial Crabmeat . 9.95
BIN NO. 32 OR 54

**BAKED DEVILED CRAB MEAT** — AU GRATIN — All Lump Crabmeat . . . 9.50
BIN NO. 37

**BREADED DEEP FRIED JUMBO FANTAIL SHRIMP** — Tartar Sauce . . . . 9.50
BIN NO. 31 OR 30

**BROILED FILET OF ATLANTIC FLOUNDER** with Lemon Butter . . . . . 8.95
BIN NO. 35

**BREADED DEEP SEA SCALLOPS** Served on Crisp Lettuce — Tartar Sauce . . . 8.95
BIN NO. 34

**FRESH BREADED LONG ISLAND OYSTERS** w/Pepper Cabbage . . . . . 8.95

# Delaware County

## Delaware County: Clifton Heights
## CLAM TAVERN
Seafood                                              $

Clam Tavern is as famous for its crowds and long waits as it is for low prices and good seafood. Waiting for a table here can mean anything from an easy 15 minutes sitting, drink in hand, to a not-so-easy hour, standing nose to nose with other uncomfortable but determined bargain diners. The menu, printed on a paper placemat, features fried fish, steamed shrimp and clams, broiled lobster tails, steak, chicken and more; all priced so low (even the drinks) you wonder how they can do it and keep up the quality. They do it with crowds, that's how.

CLAM TAVERN, 339 East Broadway Avenue, Clifton Heights, Pennsylvania. Telephone: (215) 623-9537. Hours: Monday-Thursday 4-11 pm; Friday and Saturday 4 pm-midnight. No cards. No reservations. Full bar service. Street parking.

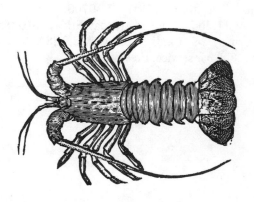

## Delaware County: Newtown Square
## NEWTOWN SQUIRE
American                                    $$

It is almost impossible to remember a time when the Newtown Squire wasn't one of the biggest, most popular restaurants in the suburbs. What keeps the parking lot full and the customers coming back for more starts with beef. The prime rib (squire cut) is a mammoth portion that almost defies you to eat it all. Most diners concede defeat and end up feeding the family on what is toted home in the people bag that the staff provides almost automatically. The rest of the menu pretty much follows suit. Much of it is geared to America's appetite for meat and shellfish. In addition to the super ribs, find pork chops, calves liver, filet mignon, double lamb chops, rack of lamb and a variety of veal dishes. Seafood is represented by a daily fresh fish choice, live lobster, lobster tails, crabmeat in several forms and scallops.

NEWTOWN SQUIRE, Route 252, Newtown Square, Pennsylvania. Telephone: (215) 356-9700. Lunch: Monday-Saturday 11:30-2. Dinner: Monday-Friday 5-10; Saturday 5-11; Sunday 2-9. Cards: AE, DC, MC, VISA. Reservations advised. Full bar service. Free parking.

# SEAFOOD & SHELLFISH

| | |
|---|---|
| **FRESH FISH OF THE DAY** Sauted in Lemon Butter | **7.00** |
| **BROOK TROUT ALMONDINE** Fresh Pennsylvania | **7.50** |
| **SQUIRE CRAB IMPERIAL** All Jumbo Lump Crabmeat | **8.50** |
| **STUFFED OYSTERS WITH CRABMEAT** | **8.50** |
| **STUFFED MUSHROOMS WITH CRABMEAT** | **8.50** |
| **BROILED SCALLOPS** Lemon Butter | **8.75** |
| **CRABMEAT SAUTEED** Backfin Jumbo Lump | **10.00** |
| **LIVE LOBSTERS** Flown in Daily From Nova Scotia Price According to Size | |
| **BROILED AFRICAN LOBSTER TAILS** Melted Butter | **16.00** |

# BEEF & SPECIALTIES

| | |
|---|---|
| **BREAST OF CAPON** Hickory Smoked Ham, Beaujolais Sauce | **7.50** |
| **VEAL PARMIGIANA** | **8.00** |
| **CALVES LIVER SAUTE** with Hickory Smoked Bacon | **8.00** |
| **STUFFED PORK CHOPS** | **7.50** |
| **PRIME LONDON BROIL** Tender Slices of Beef Au Jus | **8.00** |
| **PETITE FILET MIGNON** Sauce Bearnaise | **9.75** |
| **SELECT PRIME FILET MIGNON** Sauce Bearnaise | **12.00** |
| **SELECT PRIME SIRLOIN STEAK** Sauce Bearnaise | **12.00** |
| **BROILED DOUBLE RIB SPRING LAMB CHOPS** | **14.00** |
| **ROAST PRIME RIBS (Squire Cut)** | **12.00** |
| **ROAST RACK OF LAMB** | **16.00** |
| **SURF and TURF** | **13.50** |
| **FROG LEGS** Sauteed in Garlic Butter | **8.00** |

*Nature Veal Specialty of the Week*
*$9.95*

| | |
|---|---|
| **VEAL MARSALA** | **VEAL FRANCAISE** |
| **VEAL OSCAR** | **VEAL SORRENTO** |
| **VEAL PICANTE** | **VEAL ROBERTO** |

## Delaware County: Media
## PEKING
Chinese                                                        $

You'd expect a shopping-center Chinese restaurant to be a
chow mein palace wouldn't you? The Peking, located in
the Granite Run Mall near Media, offers, however, sam-
plings from Chinese haute cuisine along with the more
familiar favorites of Chinese-American restaurants. The
Peking kitchen produces spicy, fire-breathing specialties
from Szechwan, Shanghai-style spring rolls, Mongolian meat
and vegetable dishes (try the lamb) and, of course, Peking
duck. The latter is available at a minute's notice and, for
those whose appetites are small, there's a half-duck portion.
The restaurant's rather extensive menu also lists a special
house dinner for about $10 per person. It includes soup, a
sampling of hors d'oeuvre and one of six interesting entrées,
ranging from lobster chicken roll to steamed sea bass with
black beans and ginger root. There's also rice, tea and a
special dessert for the price.

PEKING RESTAURANT, Granite Run Mall, Routes 1 and
352, Media, Pennsylvania. Telephone: (215) 566-4110.
Hours: Monday-Thursday 11:30 am-9:30 pm; weekends to
10 pm. Cards: AE, DC, MC, VISA. Reservations advised.
No alcoholic beverages; bring your own. Free parking.

# TOWNE HOUSE
**Italian American**

**$$**

A demented Santa Claus obviously masterminded the decor here. What other reason could there be for suspending hundreds of playthings from the ceilings of the Towne House's labyrinth of rooms? Until you're accustomed to the whacky scenery overhead, you'll lift your eyes often, startled at discovering a pair of rusting ice skates next to an upturned saddle, or a smudgy plush rabbit swinging beside a real wooden duck decoy. Fortunately for everyone, gregarious owner Babe D'Ignazio takes the food more seriously than the decor. The result is a successful family restaurant that offers huge steaks, a variety of seafood specialties, grilled meats and lots of Italian pasta and parmigiana preparations. Gourmands gallop here for the two-and-a-half-pound porterhouse called "the biggest steak in town." Kids have their own menu, one that lists a choice of four hot platters, as well as sandwiches, burgers and salad. There's even a late-night snack card filled with fun foods like sandwiches, cheese and cracker trays, canapé platters, steamed clams and, for the really big snacker, spaghetti. The wine list lets you splurge on vintage Dom Perignon at $45 a bottle if that's your style, but provides many other more affordable alternatives as well.

D'IGNAZIO'S TOWNE HOUSE, 117 South Avenue, Media, Pennsylvania. Telephone: (215) 566-6141. Lunch: daily from 11:30 am. Dinner: Monday-Thursday 4 pm-10:30 pm; Friday and Saturday to midnight. Late snacks on weekends to 1 am. All major credit cards. Reservations advised. Full bar service. Street parking.

## Appetizers

| | | | |
|---|---|---|---|
| Canape of Anchovies | 2.95 | Iced Celery Hearts and Olives | 1.50 |
| Chilled Tomato Juice | 75 | Jumbo Lump Crabmeat Cocktail | 4.95 |
| Fruit Cocktail | 1.25 | Half Dozen Clams on Half Shell | 1.75 |
| Jumbo Shrimp Cocktail | 3.50 | One & a Half Dozen Steamed Clams | 3.25 |
| ANTIPASTO FOR TWO | 6.50 | Baked Clams Casino | 3.25 |
| Chopped Chicken Liver Pate | 1.75 | Fresh Chester Co. Mushrooms Stuffed with Lump Crabmeat | 3.50 |

## Soups and Stews

| | | | |
|---|---|---|---|
| Snapper | 1.25 | Italian Escarole | 75 |
| Clam Chowder | 75 | Oyster Stew (in season) | 2.95 |
| Vegetable | 75 | Clam Stew | 2.95 |

French Onion au Fromage .... 1.50

## Salads and Cold Platters

Antipasto Made To Your Order

| | |
|---|---|
| FRESH SHRIMP SALAD BOWL | 7.50 |
| LUMP CRABMEAT SALAD BOWL | 7.50 |
| SLICED HAM and POTATO SALAD PLATTER | 4.50 |
| CHEF'S SALAD BOWL JULIENNE | 4.50 |

Our Famous Salad Bowl $1.95

## Italian Specialties

| | | | |
|---|---|---|---|
| SPAGHETTI and MEAT BALLS | 4.75 | RAVIOLI and MEAT BALLS | 4.75 |
| SPAGHETTI and MUSHROOMS | 5.25 | RIGATONI and MEAT BALLS | 4.75 |
| SPAGHETTI ALIO E OLIO | 5.25 | HOMEMADE BAKED LASAGNE | 5.50 |
| SPAGHETTI—Whole Fresh Clams (red or white sauce) | 6.50 | MANICOTTI and MEAT BALLS | 4.75 |
| | | BREADED VEAL CUTLET with Spaghetti | 7.95 |
| CHICKEN, Pan Fried in Olive Oil and Garlic | 7.25 | D'IGNAZIO'S VEAL CUTLET PARMIGIANA | 8.50 |

## Steaks, Chops & Fowl

| | | | |
|---|---|---|---|
| CENTER CUT FILET MIGNON (12 oz.) | 10.95 | SOUTHERN FRIED CHICKEN | 5.95 |
| PETITE FILET MIGNON (8 oz.) | 8.95 | BROILED CHOPPED BEEF STEAK | 5.95 |
| PORTERHOUSE STEAK (2½ lbs.) | 12.50 | (2) CENTER CUT LOIN PORK CHOPS | 6.95 |
| "The Biggest Steak in Town" | | PAN FRIED CALF'S LIVER, Crisp Bacon | 6.95 |
| PRIME BONELESS SIRLOIN STRIP (1 lb.) | 9.95 | (2) DOUBLE THICK LOIN LAMB CHOPS, Minted Pear | 9.95 |
| D'IGNAZIO'S STEAK-A-BABE | 6.95 | | |

OUR FAMOUS SURF & TURF - ½ lb. Filet and (2) Lobster Tails ... 15.50
(Other Combinations to Order)

### Our Specialty Roast Prime Ribs of Beef

$9.50

## Seafood & Shellfish

| | | | |
|---|---|---|---|
| BROILED BONELESS IDAHO TROUT | 6.50 | CRAB CAKES A LA D'IGNAZIO | 7.95 |
| BROILED LOBSTER TAILS | 11.95 | JUMBO LUMP CRABMEAT au Gratin | 8.50 |
| BAKED FLOUNDER STUFFED with CRABMEAT | 7.95 | BAKED SHRIMP IMPERIAL | 9.50 |
| FRIED JUMBO BUTTERFLIED SHRIMP | 8.50 | (jumbo shrimp stuffed with crab imperial) | |
| BOUNTIFUL COMBINATION SEAFOOD PLATTER | 11.25 | BROILED FILET OF SOLE, Lemon Butter | 7.50 |
| | | SHRIMP SCAMPI | 9.95 |

PLATTERS INCLUDE: Salad, Garlic Bread, Baked Stuffed Potato, Coffee

# Lancaster County

## Lancaster County: Mount Joy
## GROFF FARM
Pennsylvania Dutch                                    $

Betty and Abe Groff run a country restaurant true to the rural area it serves. Let others plant fake buggies drawn by concrete mares in order to snare the New York tourists. The Groffs tell it like it is—or was until recently—without plastic hex signs or machine-made shoofly pie. The Groff place was once Abe and Betty's home, the fourth farm on the left on the road leading out of the pretty Lancaster-area town of Mount Joy. It's a collection of small dining rooms furnished à la Norman Rockwell, with old-fashioned wallpaper and starched curtains. It offers food so plain it just has to be good to stand the close scrutiny. The Groffs and their staff serve dinner and lunch family style. Choices include moist, full-of-flavor country ham, chicken Stoltzfus, chunks of light and dark chicken with stamp-sized pieces of crisp pastry floated in golden gravy, or fairly ordinary rib roast of beef. Meats are main events in a meal that unofficially begins with cracker pudding and chocolate cake in Pennsylvania Dutch style. You are reminded by petite Betty's booming voice to eat up or you'll break house tradition. The pudding looks like wet crackers and tastes like coconut; it's part of a quartet of relishes that includes homemade dill pickles, pickled watermelon rind and chow chow, the last a mustard vegetable relish. The real meal begins with fruit cup (the supermarket variety), with a good lemon sherbet, or hearty, ham-flecked bean soup.

Vegetables are country style—overcooked but delicious and buttery. Despite mammoth first servings that include home-made bread and butter, you are urged to take seconds of everything. Then when you can barely push your chair away from the table, you are invited to tour the cellar for a sip of the Groff's homemade sweet wine and a peek at the shelves filled with home-canned farm bounty. Groff's is understandably popular and you may find getting a reservation for the time you want difficult. Keep trying. It's worth the effort.

GROFF FARM, RD 3, Mount Joy, Pennsylvania. Telephone: (717) 653-1520. Lunch: Tuesday-Friday from 12:30. Dinner: Tuesday-Friday 5-7; Saturday 5-7:30. No cards. Reservations required. No alcoholic beverages. Free parking.

## Lancaster County: Lancaster
## JETHRO'S
Continental

**$$**

Jethro's is new, small and very much in touch with today. That wouldn't be much of a surprise if the restaurant were located in Philadelphia or New York. But Jethro's is in Lancaster, on a street where people live in houses with front porches. The restaurant's bar (which you must travel through on your way to the dining room) draws lots of attractive young people from the area. The dining room crowd is a happy mix of different ages and sexes. The walls are plywood paneled and the furnishings Spartan, but there are lots of nice touches like freshly laundered linens and fresh flower bouquets (a different combination for every table). The manageable menu offers a cold hors d'oeuvre assortment that includes egg with garlic mayonnaise, prosciutto and attractively arranged marinated vegetables. There's a pasta and broccoli combination that's available hot or cold. Both were sampled and approved at a recent meal. Entrées that checked out nicely were fresh crabmeat in creamy Mornay sauce and chicken with a sausage chestnut stuffing and cider glaze. With coffee came desserts, an interesting walnut torte and a raspberry-glazed strawberry tart. Wine, from a small, slightly unbalanced and expensive list, was a California Pinot Chardonnay.

JETHRO'S, First and Ruby Streets, Lancaster, Pennsylvania. Telephone: (717) 299-1700. Hours: Monday-Saturday 5 pm-midnight; Sunday 4 pm-8 pm; Sunday brunch noon-4 pm. Cards: MC, VISA. Reservations advised. Full bar service. Street Parking.

# Montgomery County

## Montgomery County: Gilbertsville
## FAGLEYSVILLE COUNTRY HOTEL
## International

$$

Jack Gleason calls his place a country hotel, and it looks the part. This big barn of a building is about as stylish as a sunbonnet and it's located in an area so rural Gleason says he can't get the city newspaper to deliver. All of this leaves diners totally unprepared for the Gleason kitchen, which is so worldly you may sample a different cuisine for every course. One of the standby appetizers is an order of Chinese spring rolls that are crispy and delicious enough to win a prize in Chinatown. A stellar entrée is entrecôte Madrid, sirloin sauced with a garlic-perfumed paste of walnuts and anchovies. Desserts include German cakes, French pastries and cold soufflés. The dish that lures many of Gleason's long-distance diners is the canard à la Fagleysville, a glazed duckling half made from a recipe guarded as carefully as the original formula for oysters Rockefeller. The hotel bar and wine cellar are stocked to match the quality of the cuisine.

FAGLEYSVILLE COUNTRY HOTEL, RD 1, Gilbertsville, Pennsylvania. Telephone: (215) 323-1425. Hours: dinner, 5:30 pm-9 pm; closed Monday. Cards: AE, DC, MC, VISA. Reservations advised. Full bar service. Free parking.

| | |
|---|---|
| **FILET en CROUTE** (topped with chopped mushrooms & scallion, encased in Puff Pastry & baked, served with Madeira sauce) | 14 95 |
| **ENTRECOTE MADRID** (Sirloin with a Walnut-Anchovy-Garlic sauce) | 14 95 |
| **POULET** MAISON | 8 95 |
| **POULET CORDON BLEU en CROUTE** (breast of Chicken, Ham, Swiss Cheese, baked in Puff Pastry, served with Normandy sauce) | 9 95 |
| **ORIENTAL CHICKEN PUFF** (breast of Chicken & Oriental Vegetables baked in Puff Pastry, served with Sweet & Sour sauce) | 8 95 |
| **SEAFOOD SCAMPI** (Lobster Meat, Scallops, Shrimp & Crabmeat in a Garlic, Butter & Oil Sauce) | 13 95 |
| **HOMARD CONIL** (Lobster Meat flambed with Pernod, with Mushrooms, Parsley & Scallions, cohered with Bechamel Sauce) | 14 95 |
| **FRUITS de la MER, SAUCE AURORE** (Lobster Meat, Scallops, Shrimp & Crabmeat, simmered in White Wine with Parsley & Scallions, cohered with a Cream sauce with chopped Tomatoes) | 13 95 |
| **TRUIT SOUFFLE, BUERRE de CITRON** (whole Trout stuffed with Trout Souffle, baked, served with Lemon White Butter sauce) | 13 95 |
| **HOMARD ALLAH, RICE PILLAF** (Lobster Meat flambed with Scotch, Cognac & Curacao, with fresh Orange Juice & Heavy Cream, served with Rice Pilaf). Not available on Saturdays. | 16 9. |

## Montgomery County: Radnor
## THE GREENHOUSE
International        **$$**

Once a gift shop and before that a garden supply center, this plot of Main Line prime in Radnor is far enough from busy Route 30 to keep it a secret from outsiders yet near enough to "good" addresses for it to be a luxurious neighborhood restaurant and lounge. The original building was a stable built in the 1700s; today it is a cozy hideaway dining room. Adjoining are the bar and garden rooms, the latter high-ceilinged, white-walled and colorfully decorated with patchwork tablecloths over yellow table skirts. Potted plants and candles carry out the greenhouse theme. Jutting from the main entrance is the greenhouse wing for which the place is named. Here the furnishings are hefty wrought iron and the air hangs heavy with New Orleanslike humidity amidst a jungle of plants. Greenhouse food tends to be pleasant, garden-variety stuff that doesn't detract much from the scenery. The most unusual entrée on a recent visit was veal splashed with calvados. Local favorites run to crabmeat Imperial, rack of lamb, broiled beef. Sunday brunch is often crowded and for good reason. In addition to the sunny setting, the place is one of the rare Main Line locations open for this leisurely Sunday meal. Brunch selections range from simple corn fritters and sautéed apples to the classic extravagance of eggs Florentine. There's even a children's brunch du jour. Desserts, sauces and salad dressings are all made on the premises.

THE GREENHOUSE, King of Prussia Road and Belrose Lane, Radnor, Pennsylvania. Telephone: (215) 687-2801. Lunch: Monday-Friday 11:30 am-2:30 pm. Dinner: Monday-Thursday 5:30 pm-9:30 pm; Friday and Saturday 5:30 pm-10 pm; Sunday 4 pm-7:30 pm. Sunday brunch noon-3 pm. Cards: AE. Reservations advised. Full bar service. Parking lot.

# Greenhouse Dinner Menu

## Appetizers

| | |
|---|---|
| Clams Casino | 3.25 |
| Gulf Shrimp Cocktail Lamaze | 3.75 |
| Greenhouse Pâté | 2.25 |
| Mushroom Gruyère | 2.25 |
| Fruit de Mer | 4.00 |
| Oysters Rockefeller, Bienville and Ruffignac | 5.75 |
| Escargots à la Bourguignonne | 3.75 |
| Clams on the Half Shell | 2.75 |
| Smoked Nova Scotia Salmon | 3.75 |
| Bluepoint Oysters on the Half Shell | 3.25 |

## Soups

Snapper 1.50   Baked French Onion 1.75   Soup du Jour 1.00

## Entrees

Broiled Filet Mignon, Sauce Bordelaise 11.25
Broiled Sirloin Strip Steak, Sauce Beárnaise 11.25
Sliced Filet of Beef à la Deutsch 8.50
Paul Bocuse's Lamb Curry 8.25
Duck à l'Orange 8.50
Glazed Swedish Rack of Baby Lamb 11.25
Greenhouse Cassoulet of Lobster, Shrimp and Crab 11.00
Frogs Legs Provencal 9.50
Coquilles Saint - Jacques 9.50
Chicken Soldoli 8.25
Escalope of Natured Veal Calvados 9.25
Paillard of Veal, Maitre d'Hotel 9.25
Chesapeake Crabmeat Imperial 8.75
Sauté of Fresh Scallops au Vin 8.25
Greenhouse Seafood du Jour

## Beverages

Mocha - Java Coffee .65   Sanka .50   Darjeeling Tea .50
Espresso 1.50

## Montgomery County: Lansdale
## HOTEL TREMONT
American/French $$

The Tremont is one of suburbia's long-playing success stories. This dedicated Main Street restaurant has maintained its reputation for good food for well over 30 years. Although the Tremont's fare is billed as French (a look at the menu shows category headings in that language), most items seem to be American favorites. Find broiled lamb chops, as well as surf and turf, fried scallops and breaded veal cutlet outnumbering the frogs legs provençal (very heavy on the garlic, incidentally) and French omelets. Expect decor that's more Main Street than Paris and a clientele that thinks enough of the place to dress up a bit for dinner.

HOTEL TREMONT, Main and Broad Street, Lansdale, Pennsylvania. Telephone: (215) 855-4266. Hours: 11:30 am-2:30 pm; 5 pm-10 pm; late supper 10 pm-1 am. Closed Sunday. House charges only. Reservations advised. Full bar service. Free parking. Children's menu. Pianist Wednesday, Friday and Saturday evening.

# ENTRÉES

## SPECIALITÉS DE LA MAISON

| | |
|---|---|
| Grilled Sweetbreads & Mushrooms on Toast | 8.50 |
| Veal Parmigiana | 8.00 |
| Frogs' Legs Saute Provencale | 9.00 |
| Scallops Saute with Garlic Butter on Toast | 8.00 |
| Filet of Fresh Flounder Stuffed with Crabmeat | 10.00 |

## POISSONS

| | |
|---|---|
| Deviled Back Fin Crabmeat Cake | 7.00 |
| Fried Deep Sea Scallops, Tartar Sauce | 7.00 |
| Filet of Fresh Flounder, Broiled or Saute Amandines | 8.50 |
| Fresh Back Fin Crabmeat Saute | 9.00 |
| Broiled South African Lobster Tails, Drawn Butter | 11.50 |
| Broiled South African Lobster Tails, Stuffed with Crabmeat | 13.00 |

## PLATS GARNIS

| | |
|---|---|
| Breaded Veal Cutlet, Tomato Sauce | 7.50 |
| Half Spring Chicken, Broiled or Fried | 7.00 |
| French Omelette, Cheese or Mushroom | 6.50 |
| Fresh Calves Liver Saute with Bacon | 8.00 |

## GRILLADES

| | |
|---|---|
| Broiled Rib Lamb Chops | 10.50 |
| Tremont Minute Steak | 8.50 |
| Broiled Filet Mignon with Mushrooms | 11.00 |
| Broiled Prime Sirloin Steak | 11.00 |
| Surf & Turf | 13.00 |

## LEGUMES ET SALADES (Choice of Two)

| | | |
|---|---|---|
| Apple Sauce | Browned Potatoes | Cole Slaw |
| Buttered Peas | Parsley Potatoes | Pickled Beets |
| Corn Saute | French Fried Potatoes | Sliced Tomatoes |
| Leaf Spinach | Sweet Potato | Tossed Green Salad |
| Lima Beans | | Hearts of Lettuce |

Choice of Tremont Dressings:
French, Russian, Oil & Vinegar
Crumbled Roquefort Cheese .50

## Montgomery County: Ardmore
## HU-NAN
### Chinese (Hunan)

**$**

The Hu-Nan is easily the area's most stylish Chinese restaurant as well as suburbia's only restaurant specializing in the pepper-fired cuisine of China's Hunan region. The listings inside the artistic, bamboo-design menu are fewer than you'd find in Chinatown. There are no column A and column B dinners here, only four appetizers and an equally limited number of soups. Some of the more unusual dishes are the zucchini bean curd, lemon steak and Hunan lamb, all quite spicy but delicious. More familiar fare like steak with oyster sauce, butterfly shrimp, sweet and sour pork and even fried rice and chop suey may also be ordered. The restaurant does not sell alcoholic beverages, but they will chill and uncork the wine you bring.

HU-NAN, 47 East Lancaster Avenue, Ardmore, Pennsylvania. Telephone: (215) 642-3050. Lunch: Tuesday-Friday 11:30 am-3 pm. Dinner: Tuesday-Friday 5 pm-9:30 pm; Saturday and Sunday 5 pm-10 pm. Cards: AE, DC, VISA. Reservations advised. Bring your own wine. Municipal parking lot nearby.

| APPETIZERS | Egg Roll | .95 |
|---|---|---|
| | Fried Wonton (3) | .80 |
| | Barbecued Spare Ribs (3) | 2.25 |
| | Hu-Nan Hot and Sweet Cabbage | .95 |

| SOUPS | Egg Drop | .70 |
|---|---|---|
| | Wonton | .80 |
| | Hot and Sour | .90 |
| | Shrimp and Rice Cake (for 4) | 5.25 |

| CHICKEN | | | |
|---|---|---|---|
| | 1 | Chicken with Sliced Cucumbers (spicy) | 4.95 |
| | 2 | Premier's Chicken (very spicy) | 4.75 |
| | 3 | Straw-Mushroom Chicken | 4.95 |
| | 4 | Hu-Nan Chicken (spicy) | 5.25 |

| BEEF | | | |
|---|---|---|---|
| | 5 | Steak with Oyster Sauce | 4.75 |
| | 6 | Pepper Steak | 4.75 |
| | 7 | Straw-Mushroom Steak | 4.95 |
| | 8 | Steak with Snow Peapods | 5.25 |
| | 9 | Zucchini Steak (spicy) | 5.25 |

| PORK | | | |
|---|---|---|---|
| | 10 | Yu Siang Pork (spicy) or Szechuan Pork | 4.75 |
| | 11 | Pork and Shredded Cabbage (spicy) | 4.50 |
| | 12 | Sweet and Sour Pork | 4.95 |
| | 13 | Moo Shu Pork and Pancakes | 6.25 |

| SHRIMP | | | |
|---|---|---|---|
| | 14 | Butterfly Shrimp | 5.95 |
| | 15 | Baby Shrimp with Green Peas (or Eggs) | 4.75 |
| | 16 | Shrimp with Sizzling Rice | 5.25 |
| | 17 | Shrimp with Lobster Sauce | 5.50 |
| | 18 | Shrimp with Water Chestnuts | 5.95 |

| SPECIALTIES | | | |
|---|---|---|---|
| | 19 | Zucchini Bean Curd (spicy) | 5.25 |
| | 20 | Home Style (or Ma-Pao) Bean Curd (spicy) | 5.25 |
| | 21 | Mixed Vegetables | 5.25 |
| | 22 | Mongolian Barbecue (very spicy) | 5.75 |
| | 23 | Hu-Nan Filet Mignon (spicy) | 7.25 |
| | 24 | Hu-Nan Shrimp (spicy) | 7.95 |
| | 25 | Yu Siang Shrimp (spicy) | 7.50 |
| | 26 | Crispy Duck | 7.50 |
| | 27 | Lemon Steak (very spicy) | 5.95 |
| | 28 | Yu Siang Egg Plant (spicy) | 5.75 |
| | 29 | Pork with Black Beans (spicy) | 5.75 |
| | 30 | Hu-Nan Lamb (spicy) | 7.95 |
| | 31 | Tung Ting Scallop (spicy) | 7.95 |
| | 32 | Tung Ting Lobster (spicy) | 11.95 |
| | 33 | Jade Green Lobster | 9.95 |
| | 34 | Peking Duck (Advanced Orders Only) | 20.00 |

| SIDE DISHES | Fried Rice (Pork, Shrimp, or Beef) | 3.25 |
|---|---|---|
| | Lo-Mein (Pork, Shrimp, Chicken, or Beef) | 3.95 |
| | Sum-Gum Lo-Mein | 4.50 |
| | Chop Suey (Pork, Shrimp, Chicken, or Beef) | 4.25 |

## Montgomery County: West Conshohocken
## THE INN OF THE FOUR FALLS
### American

**$$**

The Inn of the Four Falls is one of those rare restaurants-with-a-view that doesn't demand a heavy price for the scenery. This affordable eatery looks ancient but is actually of fairly recent vintage. "Instant age" was provided through hand-hewn beams that date back to the early 1700s. Views are of silvery ribboned water shimmering down a heavily wooded hillside and waterfowl that strut and splash for the benefit of onlookers. Under the most recent owner, the food has been good, simple and reasonably priced. Both prime rib and a one-and-a-half-pound broiled lobster with potato, salad bar, good bread and lots of butter cost under $7, and a variety of additional specials are available for even less. The wine list stays in the price range of the food.

THE INN OF THE FOUR FALLS, Conshohocken State Road, West Conshohocken, Pennsylvania. Telephone: (215) 878-6347. Hours: Tuesday-Saturday from 5 pm; Sunday from 2:30 pm. Closed Monday. All major credit cards. Reservations advised. Full bar service. Parking lot. Children's specials.

## Appetizers

| | |
|---|---|
| LOUISIANA GULF SHRIMP COCKTAIL | 3.00 |
| CHERRY STONE CLAMS on the Half Shell | 1.75 |
| BAKED CLAMS CASINO | 3.00 |
| FRESH FRUIT CUP SUPREME | .75 |

## Soups

| | | | |
|---|---|---|---|
| BAKED ONION SOUP SAVORYADE | | | 1.75 |
| ONION SOUP Au Cruton | .60 | SOUP du Jour | .60 |
| SNAPPER SOUP | CUP .75 | BOWL | 1.25 |

## Salads

CAESAR SALAD for TWO .......... 3.00    Blue Cheese Dressing 50¢ extra

## Entree

| | |
|---|---|
| ROAST PRIME RIB OF BEEF AU JUS | 6.50 |
| includes potato, salad bar, and beverage | |

| | |
|---|---|
| ROAST PRIME RIB OF BEEF (Extra Cut) | 9.50 |
| BROILED PRIME STRIP SIRLOIN STEAK 1 lb. | 10.50 |
| BROILED PRIME STRIP SIRLOIN STEAK 12 oz. | 9.00 |
| BROILED PRIME FILET MIGNON with Mushroom Cap | 10.50 |
| PETITE FILET MIGNON with Bordelaise Sauce | 9.00 |
| GRILLED CHOPPED TENDERLOIN STEAK with Mushroom Sauce | 4.50 |
| BROILED SHASHLEEK on Rice Pilaf with Bordelaise Sauce | 6.95 |
| FANCY BREADED VEAL CUTLET PARMIGIANA with Italian Sauce and Spaghetti | 6.50 |
| SURF and TURF: Petite Filet Mignon and Lobster Tail with Drawn Butter | 11.95 |
| BAKED BROOK TROUT with Crab Meat Dressing | 6.25 |
| BREADED JUMBO LOUISIANA GULF SHRIMP Deep Fried with Cocktail Sauce | 6.25 |
| DEEP SEA SCALLOPS, Deep Fried with Tartar Sauce or Broiled on Rice | 5.50 |
| OLD FASHIONED CRAB CAKES with Tartar Sauce | 5.95 |
| BROILED COMBINATION SEAFOOD PLATTER (Lobster Tail, Shrimp Scampi, Scallops, Flounder, Clams Casino) | 9.95 |
| BROILED JUMBO SOUTH AFRICAN ROCK LOBSTER TAIL, creamy drawn butter | 9.95 |
| BROILED SHRIMP SCAMPI with Garlic, Sherry Butter | 7.95 |
| ROAST LONG ISLAND DUCKLING on Rice Pilaf with Bordelaise Sauce | 6.95 |
| BONELESS BREAST of CAPON ROMANOFF on Rice Pilaf with Mushroom Sauce | 5.50 |

### ALL ENTREES INCLUDE:

Buffet Salad Bar                    Home Made Breads

| | | | |
|---|---|---|---|
| Baked Potato | .50 | Onion Rings | 1.00 |
| French Fried Potatoes | .50 | Mushroom Caps | 1.75 |
| Vegetable Du Jour | .50 | | |

# Montgomery County: Strafford
## L'AUBERGE
### International

$$

Years ago, L'Auberge owners Charles and Helen Wilson began paying top food talents like James Beard to develop menu specialties for their restaurant, then located in center city Philadelphia. The money proved well spent and many of the original recipes still seem fresh and appealing as served in the Wilson's elegant Main Line location. The list of L'Auberge classics is long, but from it my own favorites remain the carrot blini appetizer and the shrimp entrée. The blinis are flecked with carrot crunch, dressed with gaudy but delicious beads of red caviar and a scarf of satiny sour cream. The shrimp wear delicate coats of tempuralike batter, fried to taffeta crispness. They're accompanied with a sauce tinged with the taste of expensive imported mustard fruits. L'Auberge gives salad lovers a choice of endive and watercress, bibb lettuce and mushroom, or avocado and cherry tomato salads with their entrée. Desserts are even more varied, ranging from fresh fruit compôte to a hot lemon or chocolate soufflé. There are usually about eight different chocolate desserts on the menu as well. The restaurant is large but divided into beautifully furnished, comfortable rooms including a new atrium. Wines have never been emphasized here but the bar has a reputation for generous, well-made drinks.

**CHARLES AND HELEN WILSON'S L'AUBERGE,** Spread Eagle Village, Strafford, Pennsylvania. Telephone: (215) 687-2840. Lunch: Tuesday-Saturday noon-2:30 pm. Dinner: Tuesday-Friday 6 pm-10 pm; Saturday 6 pm-11 pm. Closed Sunday and Monday. Cards: AE, DC. Reservations advised. Free parking.

## Appetizers

| | |
|---|---|
| Shrimp with Louis Sauce .. 4.00 | Mousse of Scallops, Duglere .3.00 |
| Carrot Blini with Red Caviar and Sour Cream ..... 3.85 | Lobster Strudel ......... 4.00 |
| | Escargots ............. 3.75 |
| Crab Claw Cocktail ..... 2.50 | Fried Brie Cheese ........ 3.00 |
| Oyster Fritters, Sauce Gribiche .......... 4.00 | Curried Crabmeat in Pastry Shell ............. 4.00 |

## Soups

French Onion Soup 2.50                                 Soup du Jour 1.50

## Entrees

LUMP CRABMEAT SOUFFLE ........................... 11.50

ROLLED FRENCH CHICKEN PANCAKE, SUPREME ......... 10.25

MOUSSE OF SOLE, Sauce Hollandaise ..................... 9.25

CATCH OF THE DAY, Dill Sauce ....................... 10.25

BROILED LAMB CHOPS, Mustard Butter ................. 11.50

ROAST FILET DE BOEUF, Sauce Bearnaise ............... 12.50

MOUSSE OF SCALLOPS, Sauce Duglere ................... 9.25

BROILED U.S. PRIME SIRLOIN STEAK, Sauce Bearnaise ....... 13.00

CRISP SHRIMP, with Fruit Sauce ....................... 11.25

#### Choice of Vegetable and Salad or Two Vegetables

| | |
|---|---|
| Acorn Squash with Pineapple | Deep Fried Zucchini Squash |
| Potatoes Dauphinoise | New Bliss Potatoes with Chives |

—— ★ ——

Belgium Endive & Watercress Salad     Bibb Lettuce & Mushroom Salad
Cherry Tomato, Avocado and Boston Lettuce Salad
Roquefort Dressing 1.25

Cafe Espresso 1.75                          Irish Coffee L'Auberge 2.75

## Desserts

| | |
|---|---|
| Fresh Strawberries with Raspberry Cassis 2.85 | Ice Cream 2.00 |
| Lime Tart with Strawberries 2.50 | Grand Marnier Souffle 3.75 |
| Lemon Souffle 3.50 | Fresh Fruit Compote 2.50 |

Coffee Ice Cream with Tia Maria and Toasted Cocoanut 2.75

Poire A La Bourguignonne 2.50

Brandy Apple Omelette 3.35                    Avocado Cream Parfait 2.50

## Desserts au Chocolat

| | |
|---|---|
| Chocolate Souffle 3.50 | Chocolate Cheese Cake 2.10 |
| Chocolate Meringue Pie 2.15 | Pot de Creme 2.10 |
| Vanilla Ice Cream, Butternut Sauce 2.50 | Mousse au Chocolat 2.10 |

Pyramid au Chocolat 2.85

Rolled Chocolate Mousse Cake 2.50

## Montgomery County: West Point
## MACPHEE'S
### French/American $$

From the standpoint of decor, the big news here is the series of spectacular stained-glass windows that transform what was once an ordinary porch into an extraordinary, rainbow-walled dining room. From the standpoint of food, the pleasures include well-made standards of the steak, lobster tail and prime rib genre, with an occasional foray into something more exotic like beef Wellington. The Wellington is one of the more popular "chef's whimsies," daily specials designed to show off the chef's considerable ability. A number of customers raved about the homemade pâté that is a part of the dish and subsequently it was added to the menu as an appetizer course. Entrées arrive with a basket of fresh, hot breads that might include slices of lemon or banana loaves as well as rolls. For dessert there's pecan pie with tender pastry and chewy-nutty filling. Five menu choices are earmarked for children and senior citizens. These wee portions are priced accordingly. Wine prices are modest as well, but don't expect to find much more than the absolute basics. Do expect to find friendliness at MacPhee's. It seasons everything served.

MACPHEE'S, West Point Pike and Garfield Avenue, West Point, Pennsylvania. Telephone: (215) 699-3585. Lunch: Monday-Friday 11:30 am-2:30 pm. Dinner: Monday-Saturday 5 pm-10 pm; Sunday 3:30 pm-8:30 pm. Snacks available 10:30 pm-1:30 am. Cards: AE, MC, VISA. Reservations advised. Full bar service. Parking lot. Children's menu.

# ❧Appetizers❧

| | | | | |
|---|---|---|---|---|
| Chilled Fresh Melon in Season | | | ............ | .85 |
| Soup du Jour | Cup | .85 | Bowl | 1.25 |
| Baked French Onion Soup | | | ............ | 1.75 |
| MacPhee's Own Snapper Soup | | Cup 1.00 | Bowl | 1.75 |
| Fried Mushrooms with Béarnaise Sauce | | | ........ | 2.00 |
| Clams Monti Casino | | | ............ | 3.50 |
| Jumbo Shrimp Cocktail | | | ............ | 3.50 |
| Broiled Chicken Liver Wrapped in Bacon | | | ........ | 2.50 |
| Paté de Maison | | | ............ | 2.50 |

# ❧Specialties❧

**Chef's Whimsey**

Each day our Chef creates a special dish. Please ask about his Whim for today.

| | |
|---|---|
| **Shrimp Provençale** ............ | 6.95 |
| Sautéed Shrimp with Tomatoes and Garlic Sauce | |
| **Lump Crabmeat au gratin** ............ | 9.95 |
| Jumbo Lump Crabmeat in a light Cheese Sauce | |
| **Tournedos Béarnaise** ............ | 9.95 |
| Twin Filets wrapped in Bacon with Mushrooms and Béarnaise Sauce | |
| **Veal Cordon Bleu Sauce Cognac** ............ | 8.50 |
| Scallops of Veal stuffed with Swiss Cheese and Ham | |
| **Veal Marango with Noodles** ............ | 7.95 |
| Sautéed Veal with Tomatoes, Garlic, Mushrooms & Olives | |
| **Roast Prime Rib of Beef au jus** ............ | 9.25 |
| Friday, Saturday and Sunday only | |

# ❧Entrees❧

| | |
|---|---|
| **Sautéed Brook Trout "Grenoblois"** ............ | 7.95 |
| **Sautéed Brook Trout Stuffed with Crabmeat** ............ | 9.95 |
| **Broiled Fresh Flounder "Almondine"** ............ | 6.50 |
| **Coquilles St. Jacques** ............ | 7.25 |
| **Sautéed Scallops "Normandes"** ............ | 7.25 |
| **Broiled Lobster Tails** ............ | 10.25 |
| **Broiled Filet Mignon Garni** ............ | 8.50 |
| **Broiled New York Sirloin Garni** ............ | 7.95 |
| **Broiled Lobster and Filet Combination** ............ | 10.25 |
| **Chicken Kiev** ............ | 6.25 |
| **Coq au Vin à la dijonnaise** ............ | 6.25 |

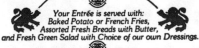

Your Entrée is served with:
Baked Potato or French Fries,
Assorted Fresh Breads with Butter,
and Fresh Green Salad with Choice of our own Dressings.

Fresh Vegetables available à la carte.

# ❧Wee Portions❧

| | |
|---|---|
| Fried Shrimp ............ | 3.50 |
| Lobster Tail ............ | 6.50 |
| Chopped Sirloin of Beef ............ | 3.95 |
| Filet Mignon ............ | 5.50 |
| Honey-Dipped Chicken ............ | 3.75 |

# Pocono Mountains

## Pocono Mountains: Canadensis
## PUMP HOUSE INN
### French

$$

If you grew up in the Pocono Mountains, as I did, you loved the tranquility and the scenery, but hated the restaurants. Until fairly recently, local folks were convinced that only fill-em-fast-and-cheap spots could survive. With the success of the Pump House, the restaurant scene shows signs of brightening. The yellow clapboard inn does very well serving sophisticated French food at city prices. (The latter are understandable when you consider that many provisions must be trucked from Philadelphia or New York.) The kitchen is more caring than imaginative. Of five appetizers listed on a recent menu, the most unusual consisted of shrimp dressed in gauzy batter, splashed with a mustard-muscled fruit sauce. Rack of lamb, which many restaurants insist was designed for couples, is available for loners here, and lamb lovers can dine solo on their own line-up of tiny, rosemary-and-parsley-scented chops. Vegetables arrive prepared in elegant country style. You might find a whole, small head of crisp cauliflower keeping company with sun-yellow slices of summer squash in a compartmented serving dish. Desserts include seasonal favorites as well as fabulous French concoctions. Arrive at blueberry time and you might be lucky enough to find a puff pastry with lightly sugared whipped cream and fresh mountain berries. Winter specialties include gâteau St. Honoré, oeufs à la neige and, on request, soufflés. The Pump House wine list offers a moderately priced range of wines that harmonize well with the food.

PUMP HOUSE INN, Sky Top Road, Canadensis, Pennsylvania. Telephone: (717) 595-7501. Hours: Wednesday-Sunday 5 pm-9 pm. Cards: AE, MC, VISA. Reservations advised. Full bar service. Free parking.

# Index

## WHERE TO EAT
## WITH YOUR LOVER

## WHERE TO EAT
## ON A BUDGET

## WHERE TO EAT WITH CHILDREN

## WHERE TO EAT LUNCH WITH THE GIRLS

## WHERE TO EAT LUNCH WITH IMPORTANT CLIENTS

## WHERE TO EAT IF YOU'VE JUST COME INTO AN INHERITANCE

## WHERE TO EAT IN BLUE JEANS

## WHERE TO EAT WITH BEAUTIFUL PEOPLE

## WHERE TO EAT WITH MUSIC

## WHERE TO EAT
## SUNDAY BRUNCH

## WHERE TO EAT
## OUTDOORS

## RESTAURANTS
## BY CUISINE

# INDEX BY GEOGRAPHY

# INDEX BY PRICE

## $

## $$$

# NOTES